HOAXES!

DUPES, DODGES & OTHER
DASTARDLY DECEPTIONS

Also from Visible Ink Press

Unexplained! 347 Strange Sightings, Incredible Occurrences, and Puzzling Physical Phenomena

Intrigue for both believer and skeptic! This intelligent and entertaining examination of strange physical phenomena analyzes some of history's most baffling events—spontaneous human combustion, phantom attackers, UFOs, crop circles, werewolves, and more. By Jerome Clark, 7.25" x 9.25" paperback, 443 pages, 100 illustrations, ISBN 0-8103-9436-7.

The Vampire Book: The Encyclopedia of the Undead

This definitive vampire guide will satisfy your thirst for vampire lore and legends from around the world with unprecedented coverage of the historical, literary, mythological, biographical, and popular aspects of one of the world's most mesmerizing subjects. Foreword by Martin V. Riccardo, founder of the Vampire Studies Network. By J. Gordon Melton, 7.25" x 9.25" paperback, 792 pages, 110 illustrations, ISBN 0-8103-2295-1.

The Astrology Encyclopedia

To meet the needs of the curious, the committed, and the casual reader, this A–Z compilation of more than 750 essays and articles covers technical, historical, and popular aspects of astrology. By James R. Lewis, 7.25" x 9.25" paperback, 630 pages, 75 illustrations, ISBN 0-8103-9460-X.

New Age Almanac

An expert's look at the personalities and significant events that have shaped and are shaping our future, from alternative medicine to "green" consumerism. By J. Gordon Melton, 6" x 9" paperback, 495 pages, illustrations, ISBN 0-8103-9402-2.

HOAXES!

DUPES, DODGES & OTHER DASTARDLY DECEPTIONS

Gordon Stein &

Marie J. MacNee

VISIBLE INK PRESS

DETROIT   WASHINGTON, D.C.

HOAXES!

DUPES, DODGES & OTHER
DASTARDLY DECEPTIONS

Published by Visible Ink Press™
a division of Gale Research Inc.
835 Penobscot Building
Detroit, MI 48226-4094

Visible Ink Press is a trademark of Gale Research Inc.

Cover photo of Orson Welles courtesy of Archive Photos; cover photo of "Invasion of the Body Snatchers" courtesy of Photofest.

Most Visible Ink Press™ books are available at special quantity discounts when purchased in bulk by corporations, organizations, or groups. Customized printings, special imprints, messages, and excerpts can be produced to meet your needs. For more information, contact Special Markets Manager, Visible Ink Press, 835 Penobscot Bldg., Detroit, MI 48226. Or call 1-800-776-6265.

Art Director: Mary Krzewinski
Illustrator: Kyle Raetz

ISBN 0-7876-0480-1

Printed in the United States of America
All rights reserved

10 9 8 7 6 5 4 3 2 1

Contents

Weird Creatures and Visitors from Beyond
- - -

Saints, Spirits, and Supernatural Scams

— — —

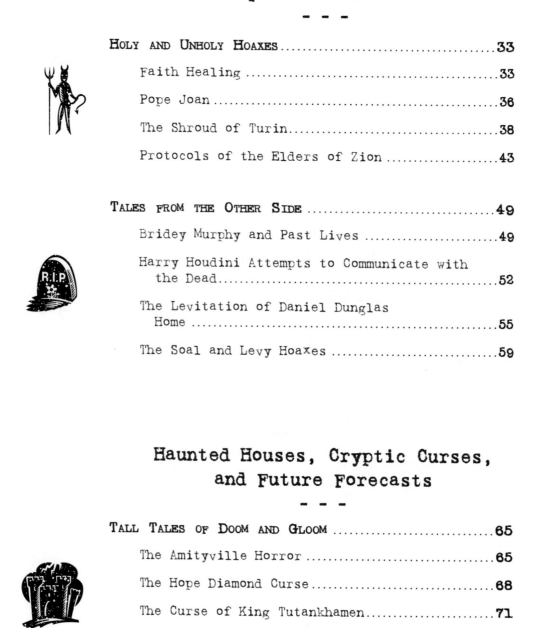

Haunted Houses, Cryptic Curses, and Future Forecasts

— — —

Globe-Trotting and Gallivanting

- - -

Military Maneuvers

- - -

Weird Science and Bad Medicine

- - -

You Can't Believe Everything You Read
- - -

Seeing Isn't Always Believing
- - -

There's No Business Like Show Business
- - -

Good Sports and Sore Losers

- - -

Heroes, Bad Guys, and Impostors

- - -

Martians, Zombies,
and Fabricated Feathers

- - -

Introduction

Haunted houses, lake monsters, flying saucers, and deadly death rays. Who hasn't heard of the Bermuda Triangle, the Loch Ness Monster, or the Amityville Horror? Yet how many people know the real story? Was Silence Dogood Ben Franklin's feminine pen name? Has Elvis Presley booked a return engagement to the world of the living? Is the Loch Ness Monster really an otter? Enquiring minds want to know.

What exactly *is* a hoax?

Cons, humbugs, scams, dupes, dodges, and deceptions—hoaxes by any other name—involve fooling at least *some* of the people *some* of the time. *Webster's Unabridged Dictionary* (10th ed.) defines a hoax as "an act intended to trick or dupe; something accepted or established by fraud or fabrication." Well, that's a start. Guido Franch was definitely up to mischief when he asked automobile companies to pay him $10 million for a secret fuel formula they could neither see nor test before they paid him. Ben Franklin had a practical joke in mind when he announced—six years prematurely—that a rival almanac writer had died. And Daniel Dunglas Home used more than a little deception to fool people into believing he was floating in thin air.

A successful hoax must be at least a *little* bit believable. Hitler *could* have escaped from his bunker on April 30, 1945. Jack the Ripper *might* have been a doctor who routinely executed the witnesses to a royal scandal. The boy King Tut *might* have cursed all who crashed his kingly catacomb. Then again, maybe not. Often, a good hoax relies on the listener's preconceived notions. Think about it: How many people would have spotted a single sea serpent in Scotland if no one had ever heard of the Loch Ness Monster? Most hoaxes work because *somebody somewhere* is ready and willing to believe the less than believable.

Does a hoaxer want the hoax to be discovered?

Never; always; sometimes. It depends. Some hoaxes bloom *after* they've been discovered. Take, for instance, George Plimpton's piece about pitching prodigy Sidd Finch that appeared in an April Fools' Day issue of *Sports Illustrated*. The fact is, there *was* no Sidd Finch; that was the point. If no one had discovered that Finch was a phantom, then the article—filled with phoney photographs and bogus biography—would have had no point.

At other times, publicity destroys the hoax. Ferdinand Demara, known as "The Great Impostor," enjoyed quite a career as a surgeon, a priest, a naval officer, and a number of other occupations that struck his fancy. When *Life* magazine published a portrait of the impostor, however, Demara's career options were soon severely limited.

What *isn't* a hoax?

Are hoaxes sometimes motivated by financial gain? Yes, indeed. But a hoax—unlike a swindle—is not *based* on the financial return. The master forger Hans van Meegeren, for example, managed to earn a tidy sum by forging the works of famous artists. The money, however, was simply a perk. The second-hand artist had quite another motive in mind: He wanted to force a group of art critics to dine on humble pie—and he succeeded, in spades.

Dozens of Dupes, Dodges & Deceptions!

Hoaxes have been perpetrated in almost every field. Here you will find political pranks, literary lies, supernatural scams, religious ripoffs, historical humbugs, scientific swindles, infamous impostors, and more. Few areas are immune from hoaxes, and the more sensitive the area, the more likely that the hoax will be memorable.

A hoaxer, without exception, *purposely intends* to deceive people. Carlos Allende, who called his UFO stories "the craziest [sic] pack of lies" he ever told, was a card-carrying hoaxer. But not everyone with a wacky take on reality is. Not every tale of Venusian visitors and Elvis encounters is perpetrated by a hoaxer. Some are created by certified cranks—eccentrics who *believe* that what they're saying is *true*.

Not every hoax started out as a hoax. Christopher Columbus had no idea when he died that his grave would inspire centuries of squabbling. Nor did Nostradamus know that his predictions—intended to cover local events in the immediate future—would be used by a Nazi astronomer to predict Germany's victory in World War II. Hoaxes sometimes gather momentum as time goes by.

Some notably intriguing affairs—which you'll find discussed in the final chapter—were not hoaxes at all. They were identified as hoaxes, or were widely believed to have been hoaxes, but were later proven not to be hoaxes. The first fossil of what was later called an Archeopteryx—a discovery that had great impact on the then-novel theory of evolution—was called a fake by disapproving scientists. Much of the scientific community became outraged by the supposed hoax—until tests proved that the fossil was indeed authentic. Perhaps the most famous "non-hoax" was the "War of the Worlds" broadcast by Orson Welles. Statements at the beginning of the broadcast made it clear that the radio show was not intended to deceive, but the panic that ensued showed that hundreds of listeners were, in fact, duped.

What you'll find here

Hoaxes! Dupes, Dodges & Other Dastardly Deceptions recreates scores of history's most interesting deceptions. Some of these hoaxes are extremely clever, funny, or outrageous. Others have changed the course of world history. Some started out as mere pranks, but got out of hand. Still others seem to have no discernable motivation. With each of the hoaxes presented here, we delineate not only the course of events, but also (when possible) the motivation of the perpetrators. And while in some cases the motivations may not be discernable, we can still enjoy these hoaxes for their cleverness or humor.

We should never lose sight of the fact that reading about hoaxes is supposed to be *fun*. There are some very clever, humorous, and rather wicked hoaxes in this book. We hope that they are as much fun to read as they were to write about.

Acknowledgments

Material for *Hoaxes! Dupes, Dodges & Other Dastardly Deceptions* was culled from Gordon Stein's *Encyclopedia of Hoaxes,* published by Gale Research Inc. For their kind assistance, we wish to thank Marcello Truzzi, James Randi, Jerry Clark, Joe Nickell, Denis Dutton, Arnold Bruce Levy, C. J. Scheiner, Robert Gutchen, Robert Weisbord, David Salamie, Larry Baker, Chris Nasso, Peg Bessette, Carol Nagel, Kathleen Witman, Christa Brelin, Kathleen Dauphinais, Margaret Chamberlain, Pam Hayes, Barbara Yarrow, Mary Krzewinski, Marco Di Vita, Judy Haughton, Vicki Burnett, Marie Rudd, Martha Ott, Ken Morse, Geoffrey Gibbs, Klaus Baernthaler, Charles Daniel, the late D. Scott Rogo, Jan Harold Brunvand, Silvia Berti, Richard H. Popkin, Richard J. Wolfe, Mark Oliver, and Judith A. Sundell.

Photographs and illustrations appearing in *Hoaxes!* were received from the following sources: Brown Brothers: **pp. 4, 16, 73, 122, 129, 174**; AP/Wide World Photos: **pp. 7, 10, 18, 39, 42, 44, 66, 70, 78, 87, 110, 115, 157, 158, 166, 183, 186, 209**; Courtesy of Dr. Gordon Stein: **pp. 15, 69, 92, 98, 103, 117, 148, 164**; Mary Evans Picture Library: **pp. 14, 26, 57, 76, 100**; Archive Photos/Popperfoto: **p. 23**; The Bettmann Archive: **pp. 37, 88, 131, 160, 180, 182, 189, 203, 205**; UPI/Bettmann: **pp. 46, 53, 84, 146, 178, 190, 207, 208**; UPI/Bettmann Newsphotos: **p. 50**; By permission of Syndics of Cambridge University Library: **p. 58**; *The Courier Journal:* **p. 74**; Archive Photos: **cover and pp. 154, 214**; Lane Stewart/Sports Illustrated: **p. 167**; Culver Pictures, Inc.: **p. 175**.

Weird Creatures
and Visitors
from Beyond

THE CARDIFF GIANT

The Cardiff Giant—a large stone figure of a human that was supposed to be a fossilized man—is one of the best-known American hoaxes. This is a tale of deceit that spans from New York to Chicago and involves more than a little ill-gotten money.

New York Cigar Maker
Unearths Giant Fossil Man!

George Hull, a cigar maker from Binghamton, in upstate New York, had a brother-in-law named William C. Newell, who had a farm near Syracuse, New York, in a town called Cardiff. In October 1869, Hull asked Newell to dig a well on his property, exactly twenty feet behind his barn. This was an unusual place to put the well, but Newell agreed. He hired two local men, and on October 16 they began to dig. Only three feet into the project, their shovels struck stone—the shape of which looked like a huge human foot. Soon, they uncovered the naked body of a ten-foot, anguished-looking stone giant.

Wasting no time, Newell bought a large tent and charged fifty cents per person to view the stone man and hear a fifteen-minute talk. Included in the price was a question-and-answer period for those who required further explanation of the giant's mysterious background.

Business was booming. Even though Newell's farm was not easy to reach, people from all over the northeast took the train to Syracuse, then rode by wagon to the Cardiff bigtop. Soon, stagecoaches ran daily from Syracuse to Cardiff. The giant, still exhibited in the pit where it was "found," drew an average of 300 to 500 visitors every day (and as many as 2,600 on one Sunday). However, even with $12,000 worth of receipts lining their pockets, Newell and Hull weren't satisfied to let the sleeping giant lie. They sold an interest in the "fossil" to some area businessmen—adding another $30,000 to their growing bank account—and on November 5, the stone man found a new home in Syracuse. Even more people flocked to see the Cardiff

Giant once the New York Central Railroad arranged a special ten-minute stop so that passengers could step across the street to view the statue.

The experts are fooled. Several experts on fossils and ancient humans paid the giant a visit. One of the first, Dr. John F. Boynton, noted that until the Cardiff Giant appeared, there had been no earlier evidence to suggest that human or animal flesh could turn to stone. The giant, he concluded, must be a statue that was carved by early Jesuit missionaries to impress the Indians. Professor James Hall, an expert in the study of rock, agreed that the stone creature was indeed a statue.

The local newspapers carried arguments for both sides. Those who opposed the statue theory pointed out that the giant was not supported by a pedestal. They also noted that a naked man writhing in agony was, to say the least, an odd subject for a sculpture. Those who argued the other side pointed to the natural striations that indicated the giant had been carved from a single block of stone.

Sleeping giant, or shameless scam?

Othniel C. Marsh, a Yale University expert on fossils, took one look at the statue and dismissed it as "a most decided humbug." In his report, he wrote, "It is of very recent origin.... I am surprised that any scientific observers should not have at once detected the unmistakable evidence against its antiquity." Marsh, unlike the other experts, had noticed the fresh tool marks and the presence of smooth, polished surfaces, which would have been roughened had the statue been buried for any length of time. Another look at the statue, and Dr. Boynton agreed. Soon, the pieces to the puzzle began to fall together.

The genesis of the hoax. In the Book of Genesis, it is written, "there were giants in the earth in those days." After arguing with a clergyman over the meaning of this passage, Hull decided to find a little fun and fortune. He purchased a very large block of gypsum—a mineral suitable for sculpting—from quarry workers in Iowa. Then he secretly shipped it to Chicago, where it was carved by two men (who later confessed to the act). Next, he shipped it by train to a depot near Binghamton, New York. The crate made its way over backroads by wagon to Newell's farm in Cardiff. After the Onondaga County Bank reported that Newell had withdrawn a sizable sum from his account (the payee: one George Hull), people began to remember that, a year earlier, they saw a large, mysterious wooden box being hauled by wagon over the backroads south of Cardiff. Hull had buried the statue behind Newell's farm one year before it was "discovered."

Hull "aged" the stone giant with acid, and created "pores" in the skin by hammering the giant with a mallet studded with needles. The giant's Cardiff burial site was in an area where many fossils and relics—real ones, that is— had been found.

Beating the Competition: P. T. Barnum, the founder of the circus in America, offered to lease the Cardiff Giant for $60,000. Refused, he had his own copy carved, which he displayed only two blocks from the Apollo Hall, where the original was exhibited. Due to the legendary circus man's promotional skills, the imitation fake drew even more people than the "real" fake.

The public remains fond of the fake. The public continued to be fascinated by the Cardiff Giant even after it had been exposed as a hoax. The statue was moved to New York City, where crowds flocked to the Apollo Hall to see it. Moved to Boston, Massachusetts, in February 1870, the giant remained in the limelight. In the following years, the statue showed up at the Pan-American Exposition in Buffalo, New York, and toured in small carnivals and state fairs around the country. In the 1930s, publisher Gardner Cowles purchased the statue, which he kept in his home in Des Moines, Iowa, until the New York State Historical Association finally persuaded him to sell the well-traveled giant. The statue changed hands in 1948, and was transferred to the Farmer's Museum in Cooperstown, New York, where it remains on display.

THE PILTDOWN MAN
- - - -

Between 1911 and 1915, a jawbone and some skull segments were discovered in Piltdown, England. Supposed to be the remains of a human-like ancestor of man, the bones were the subject of many books and articles. Today, no one questions that the Piltdown Man was created as a deliberate hoax, but why a counterfeit ancestor was created is a mystery that remains buried at Piltdown.

Orangutan Jawbone Fools Scientific Community!

In 1953—after the public had been deceived for nearly four decades—Joseph Weiner discovered that the Piltdown Man was a hoax. Weiner, an anthropologist, proved that the bones had not belonged to an ancient human ancestor; rather, the Piltdown fragments consisted of part of an orangutan jawbone and a fairly recent human skull.

Piltdown Suspects: A number of individuals, ranging from fossil collectors to a priest, have been suspected of being involved in the Piltdown hoax. Many of these men were rivals, and any one or a combination of them could have created the scam. Why? Perhaps it was jealousy. Perhaps it was the desire for fame. Perhaps it was a simple desire to sit back and enjoy the show. Among the suspects are **Sir Arthur Keith,** a famous anatomist; **Pierre Teilhard de Chardin,** a Jesuit priest and paleontologist; **Lewis Abbott,** a fossil collector; **Martin Hinton,** a zoologist; **Arthur Smith Woodward,** an anatomist; **Sir Arthur Conan Doyle,** a doctor and creator of the Sherlock Holmes character; **Grafton Elliot Smith,** an anatomist; **Frank Barlow,** a museum technician; and **William Johnson Sollas,** a geologist.

The list of suspects was long, but most of the evidence pointed to Charles Dawson, who had discovered the first fossil specimens. An amateur paleontologist, Dawson had obtained the specimens either by trading with other collectors or by purchasing them. Together with Lewis Abbott, a fossil collector, Dawson experimented with chemically aged bone specimens. Dawson involved Abbott so Dawson would have someone to accuse if the hoax prematurely came to light.

Dawson went to great pains to make sure that his hoax was not easily discovered. It seems he stole a medieval orangutan jawbone which—after a few adjustments—became the Piltdown Man's fake jawbone. First he broke off the condyle (where the jaw joins the skull) because it would easily identify the jawbone as that of an ape. Then he filed the teeth to make them look human. (Since humans and apes con-

Replicas of the Piltdown Man labeled an unscrupulous hoax by British scientists on display in the American Museum of Natural History in New York City.

sume different diets, their teeth wear differently.) Lastly, Dawson "aged" the fragments by staining the bone with potassium dichromate (often used as a dye) and treating the unusually thick human skull with other chemicals.

The stage is set. Dawson buried the bones in a gravel pit near Piltdown. He then told a couple of his collector friends that workmen digging for gravel

in the pit found an object "something like a coconut." That was all most of the collectors needed to hear: The "Heidelberg Jaw" and other remains of early human ancestors had been discovered throughout Europe, but no such fossils had been found in Great Britain. The stage was set for a British find.

Evidence of skullduggery mounts. Dawson acquired a human skull in 1906 and showed pieces of a human skull—probably the Piltdown skull—to others between 1908 and 1911. But a little math demonstrates that Dawson's story doesn't add up: the first Piltdown remains weren't discovered until 1911. What's more, sometime around 1910, Dawson asked chemist Samuel Woodhead how to treat a bone to make it appear older. Fossil collector Lewis Abbott then soaked some of Dawson's skull pieces in potassium dichromate "to harden them."

Peking Man Changes Scientists' Beliefs:

The discovery of the Peking Man's remains, as well as several other fossil finds, showed that the primitive jaw of the Piltdown Man looked odd when placed alongside the rather modern Peking skull. Discovered in an abandoned quarry near Peking, China, and identified in 1926, the Peking fossils stirred up a great deal of controversy and revolutionized what scientists believe about the history of human evolution.

In May 1913, Guy St. Barbe and Reginald Marriot, two amateur archaeologists, observed Dawson experimenting with pieces of bone soaked in chemical solutions. They kept their doubts to themselves, but Weiner's 1953 investigation indicated that not everyone believed in the Piltdown Man. Late in 1913, William King Gregory, an anatomist at the American Museum of Natural History, also voiced doubt about Dawson's remarkable discovery. Although he eventually endorsed the find as genuine, he changed his mind several times about the fossils.

Weiner unearthed the hoax with the help of anthropologist Kenneth Oakley, whose chemical analysis of the bones showed staining by potassium dichromate. The two scientists also discovered that a tooth—which had been found later at the site and was supposed to be part of an elephant molar—was in fact a modern ape tooth that had been painted with brown artist's pigment. Additionally, a "fossil" elephant bone, found later in the pit by workers, had been cut with a steel knife—not a likely choice of cutlery in the Paleolithic past.

Dawson takes his motive to the grave. Why did Dawson bury the fake remains of a phoney prehistoric man? The answer was buried with him when he died suddenly in 1916. Some believe he wanted to be respected as a scientist and accepted as a member of the Royal Society. Ironically, his Piltdown Man remains the longest held and most deceptive hoax in paleontology.

BIGFOOT HOAXES

The existence of a large, hairy, two-footed primate—known as Bigfoot, Sasquatch, Alma, the Yeti, the Wildman, and the Abominable Snowman—remains an unsolved mystery. Reports of Bigfoot sightings, which have come from all over the United States and other countries, are not all hoaxes. Many, however—such as the 1977 sighting of a man in a gorilla suit in Mission, British Columbia, Canada—are bald-faced frauds.

Humongous Feet Leave Trails of Questions!

In the United States, the description of what has been seen or found is fairly consistent. Usually, a sighting reports a seven- or eight-foot-tall biped with brownish-red fur (although some reports indicate tan or black fur) and a strong, foul odor.

Footprints have been the most common evidence of Bigfoot. In 1982, at the age of eighty-six, Rant Mullens admitted that he had been leaving bigfoot footprints in the Pacific Northwest for some fifty years. A man of modest shoe size, Mullens used bigfoot "feet" carved from wood. The experts, however, aren't buying the hoaxer's story. A foot carved from wood, even if worn as a shoe by a heavy man, will not leave impressions that are as deep or as three-dimensional as the prints that have been found. A number of Bigfoot authorities boast of having no trouble recognizing a footprint made by a carved piece of wood.

Wildman Sweeps Woman off Her Feet!

On May 2, 1976, four witnesses said that they saw a large, hairy, ape-like animal carry off a blonde woman from a wooded area outside Eureka, California. According to these witnesses, the animal was, in a word, smelly. The woman—variously identified as twenty-three-year-old Sherie Darvell, Cherie Darvell, and Sherry Nelson—was part of a television crew attempting to film footage of the big-footed one.

Unwitting Conspirators: We may never know the exact role of the other suspects in the hoax. Dawson's fellow scientist and acquaintance Martin Hinton may have detected the hoax early and, in an attempt to show Dawson that he knew what was going on, might have planted the fake elephant bone and tooth as obvious hoaxes. When they, too, were taken as serious finds, he might simply have remained silent. Teilhard de Chardin may also have become involved innocently at first, and then, realizing that he was trapped as a coconspirator, might have played along with the hoax.

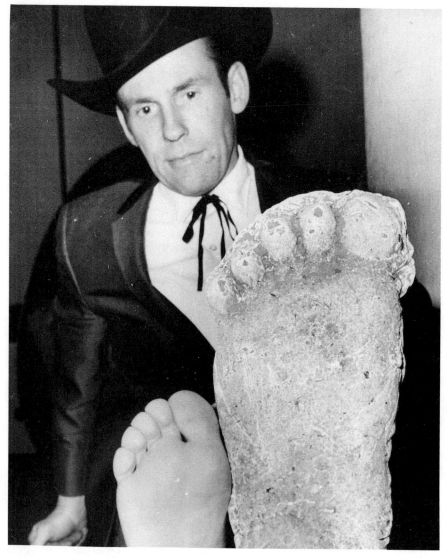

Photographer Roger Patterson compares his foot with a cast he says he
made of a big-footed beast near Eureka, California (1967).

The police began their search. If true, this incident would be the first
recorded case of the abduction of a human woman by a bigfoot. Two days
later, however, the missing woman turned up outside a resort five miles from
the site of her supposed abduction. The sheriff, who was not amused, reported that the woman was in good shape but was missing a shoe. And the woman

did little to shed light on her supposed ordeal: When reporters questioned her, she screamed.

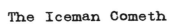

The Iceman Cometh

The "Minnesota Iceman" was supposedly a bigfoot who had been preserved in a block of ice. Exhibited for years in a refrigerated case at small carnivals around the country, the Iceman didn't cause much of a stir; that is, not until biologist Bernard Heuvelmans got wind of the frozen figure. Considered to be the father of cryptozoology, Heuvelmans spent two days with biologist Ivan Sanderson examining the body through the ice. Not easily fooled, he was convinced that the Iceman was an authentic biological specimen, possibly a Neanderthal man.

John Napier, a primatologist, took one look at Heuvelmans' sketches and notes and concluded that the Iceman was neither a Neanderthal nor a Bigfoot, but a fraud.

Frank Hansen owned the Iceman, but his account of where he got it and why it appeared to have been shot through the eye didn't make sense. Gene Emery, on the other hand, uncovered a story that did make some sense. A science reporter for Rhode Island's *Providence Journal,* Emery discovered that Howard Ball, a modelmaker for Disney Studios, confessed to his wife (who was a widow when Emery spoke to her) that he had created the Iceman at his studio in California. Eventually, Iceman owner Hansen admitted to the reporter that Ball had made an Iceman figure for him.

Evidence of a Wildman: Bigfoot reports agree that the creature is quite heavy, which causes it to leave large, deep footprints. There are reports of footprints, as well as hair samples, "scats," recordings of vocalizations, and even a few films. Outside the United States, what are supposed to be scalps and hands of Yetis are preserved in monasteries in Tibet, China; there are, however, no skulls or skeletons.

Little Bigfoot

"Jacko" was the name given to a small Bigfoot that was supposedly captured in 1884 in British Columbia, Canada. The creature—who was four feet, seven inches tall and weighed 127 pounds—might have been a chimpanzee, but he clearly didn't belong in the woods of Canada.

Only the July 4, 1884 issue of *Daily British Colonist* published the story of Jacko. The paper claimed that the creature was being held in the local jail, waiting to be sent in a cage by train to eastern Canada. That's not, however, the story that Bigfoot investigator John Green told. According to an article he

found in another newspaper (the *Mainland Guardian* of July 9, 1884), the entire story—including the part that claimed that Jacko could be viewed at the Yale, British Columbia, jail—was a complete hoax. Hoax or no hoax, crowds flocked to the jail to view the creature. This did not amuse the town jailer, who knew nothing about a hairy biped in his quarters.

Big-Footed Woman

Perhaps the most famous Bigfoot report that has been called a hoax is the Roger Patterson film of a female Bigfoot. Patterson made the twelve-second film in October 1967, near Bluff Creek in northern California. As he rode on horseback in a deep woods, more than twenty-five miles from the nearest road, he spotted a female Bigfoot. He leapt from his horse, took his movie camera out of his saddlebags, and managed to shoot thirty feet of film before the creature disappeared into the woods.

"Goodyear" Boots? In 1978 or 1979, a pair of boots was found in Stone County, Arkansas. The boots had pieces of rubber tire cut in the shape of large feet attached to the soles. Experts said the bigfoot tire prints wouldn't fool them for long.

The film has been analyzed by all sorts of "experts," whose opinions range from "obvious fake" to "definitely not a man in a monkey suit."

SEA SERPENT AND
LAKE MONSTER HOAXES

- - - -

For hundreds of years, there have been hundreds of sightings (by experienced sailors) of what appear to be sea serpents. There have also been many sightings of what seem to be very large creatures in Loch Ness in Scotland and in other large lakes all over the world. Many sightings have been discounted as hoaxes; others are mysteries that have yet to be solved....

Terrifying Lake Creatures
Lurk in Murky Scottish Waters!

Many Loch Ness "sightings" have been accompanied by photographs. Although it is impossible to say whether all Loch Ness photos are hoaxes, there is no question that some are fakes. Probably the most famous of all Loch Ness monster photos is the one called the "Surgeon's Photo," taken by Robert Kenneth Wilson, a British doctor, in 1934. Since he did not want his name associated with the photo (a tipoff, perhaps, that a scam was underway), the picture was dubbed the Surgeon's Photo.

The Surgeon's Photo shows what appears to be a neck and some kind of small head sticking out of the water; it also shows a bit of what seems to be the back of the creature. The surface of the water appears to be rippled by small waves, and the creature seems to be breaking the water as it moves. Wilson, who shunned all publicity and interviews about the photo, never claimed that his photo showed the Loch Ness Monster. The doctor claimed only that the picture he had taken in 1934 was of an object moving in Loch Ness.

Wilson took the photograph on a quarter-plate camera with what he described as a telephoto lens. At about 7:30 a.m., probably on April 19th, Wilson stopped on the road surrounding the lake. From his vantage point,

some 100 feet above the lake, he noticed a commotion about 200 to 300 yards
out. Something—he didn't say what—raised what appeared to be its head out
of the water. After running back to his car to get his camera, Wilson snapped
four pictures of the creature before it disappeared below the water. Only two
of the photographs showed anything, one of which was somewhat fuzzy and
poorly lit.

The negative of the Surgeon's Photo has been lost and the published versions of the photograph have been drastically cut down in size. Not long ago,
however, a man by the name of Stewart Campbell did a thorough analysis of a
recently discovered full-original print of the best photo. This picture offered a
new perspective on the Surgeon's Photo: Campbell's analysis shows that if the
photo had been taken from where Wilson says it was, the object would be only
0.75 meters (28 inches) long! The photo, Campbell concludes, is probably of
an otter's tail; otters, it seems, do exist in Loch Ness.

Surgeon's Photo a fake. In March 1994, Loch Ness researchers Alastair Boyd and David Martin announced that the monster in the Surgeon's Photo is a fake. Christian Spurling, the last surviving hoax conspirator, told the two researchers just before he died in November 1993 that the monster was really the head of a fake sea serpent attached to a toy submarine. Spurling explained that filmmaker Marmaduke Wetherell came up with the hoax, which involved Robert Wilson; Wetherell's son, Ian; and Spurling, Wetherell's stepson. And the dimensions of the ersatz Nessie weren't exactly daunting: the submarine-powered sea serpent stood only one foot high and eighteen inches long.

Seasick Sailors Spot Sea Serpent

In 1848, the American brig *Daphne* was unwittingly involved in a sea monster hoax. The master of the ship *Mary Ann* reported that he encountered the

Gesner's
Fischbuch.

Daphne just outside Portugal's Lisbon Harbor. The *Daphne*'s crew, according to this captain, had just seen a huge sea serpent, which they had repelled by firing spike nails and scrap iron from a deck gun.

The captain's letter was published in the *London Times*. Skeptics soon pointed out that the *Daphne* could not possibly have gotten from the latitude where the serpent was encountered to Lisbon in ten days, unless, of course, the serpent had towed the ship. Another newspaper article noted that no ship by the name of *Mary Ann* had recently been in Glasgow, Scotland, as its supposed captain had claimed. The captain, the *Mary Ann,* and the sea serpent, it seems, were the work of a journalist with a lively imagination.

Sea serpents--fact or fantasy?

CARLOS ALLENDE HOAXES THE NAVY

- - - -

O ne of the most successful unidentified flying object (UFO) hoaxes of all time was created by an eccentric drifter who sometimes used the name Carlos Miguel Allende. Born in Springdale, Pennsylvania, on May 31, 1925, Carl Meredith Allen spent most of his life wandering the United States and Mexico. According to his family, however, he dwelled permanently in a make-believe world of fantasy. Three items saved Allen from slipping into history unnoticed: two letters to author Morris K. Jessup, and an annotated copy of a paperback edition of Jessup's *The Case for the UFO* (1955).

Pennsylvania Man Encounters Hostile Aliens and Invisible Ships!

Jessup received the first of the letters in October 1955; the second one followed in January. Written in different colors of pen and pencil, and spelled erratically, they hinted that the writer—who identified himself both as Allen and Allende—knew all kinds of mysterious secrets about levitation and other matters. These other matters included the Philadelphia Experiment—a supposed 1943 experiment in which the United States Navy tested a device that used "electronic force fields" to make a battleship disappear. According to Allen's letter, the experiment resulted in

complete invisibility of a ship, Destroyer type, and all of its crew, While at sea.... Half of the officers and the crew of that Ship are at Present, Mad as Hatters.... The Experimental Ship Disappeared from its Philadelphia Dock and only a Very few Minutes Later appeared at its other Dock in the Norfolk, Newport News, Portsmouth area.... BUT the ship then, again, Disappeared And Went Back to its Philadelphia Dock in only a Very few Minutes or Less.

Gypsy notes of hostile aliens. Jessup assumed that Allen was a crank and thought nothing more about him until a year later, when he

received an invitation to the Office of Naval Research (ONR) in Washington, D.C. While there, Jessup learned that in the summer of 1956 someone had mailed an annotated copy of his book *The Case for the UFO* to the ONR office. The notes hinted that the authors, supposedly three gypsies, knew all about the secrets of UFO beings called "S-Ms" and "L-Ms." And they knew that "S-Ms" were hostile toward the human race.

Allen's prank impressed some of the junior officers, who studied the notes carefully; they wanted Jessup's opinion on the foreboding notes about alien creatures. The author took one look at the notes and—thanks to a reference to the invisibility experiment in Philadelphia (among other things)—recognized that Allen had lent a hand in the writing.

The Varo Company of Garland, Texas, ran a small printing of Allen's letters and *Case* notes. The "Varo edition" included an unsigned introduction (written by ONR Special Projects Officers Commander George W. Hoover and

Captain Sidney Sherby) that explained, "Because of the importance which we attach to the possibility of discovering clues to the nature of gravity, no possible item, however disreputable from the point of view of classical science, should be overlooked."

A sinister government plot. On April 20, 1959, Jessup, who was troubled over a failed marriage and financial problems, committed suicide in a Florida park. Rumor spread overnight: The author had been murdered by sinister government forces because of what he had learned about the Philadelphia Experiment and other mysteries hinted at in the Allende letters and the Varo edition. Allen's writings—bizarre as they were—soon took center stage as rumor kindled the public's interest.

The legend continued to grow in the 1960s, spurred by numerous publications. A 1968 cover of *New UFO Breakthrough* announced, "Our concept and understanding of flying saucers are totally wrong! So say the bizarre and terrifying ALLENDE LETTERS." The public was hooked. That same year, *The Allende Letters* appeared in a magazine format anthology. Two best-sellers, *The Bermuda Triangle* (1974) and *The Philadelphia Experiment* (1979), by William L. Moore and Charles Berlitz, brought the tale to a large popular audience that had never heard it before. Allen's flights of fancy even hit the silver screen, when New World Pictures released *The Philadelphia Experiment* in 1984.

A crazy pack of lies. The legend, it seems, had taken on a life of its own: Allen had admitted to the hoax back in 1969 when he called on Jim and Carol Lorenzen, a Tucson, Arizona, couple who were the directors of the Aerial Phenomena Research Organization (APRO). The Lorenzens, who had never taken the "Allende affair" seriously, were hardly interested in talking to the "legendary" Carlos Allende.

Nevertheless, Allen admitted to them that he, not gypsies, had made the notes in the Varo edition. His written statement said it all: He admitted that his claims in the book were "false ... the crazyest [sic] pack of lies I ever wrote." Later, however, he changed his mind to say that his confession—not the book—had been a crazy pack of lies.

Behind the Flying Saucers--Con Men and B-Movies:

In 1950, *Variety* magazine columnist Frank Scully wrote a book called *Behind the Flying Saucers*. In it, he wrote that in the late 1940s, the U.S. government had recovered the remains of three crashed spaceships and their small but humanlike Venusian passengers. The gullible writer based his book on the word of two people, Silas Newton--a "prominent oil man"--and Leo A. GeBauer--a "world-class scientific expert on magnetics," or so Scully thought. Newton and GeBauer were actually lifelong con men who were attempting to sell a bogus oil-detection device that was based, they said, on technological secrets learned from the saucers.

In 1980, Allen's parents discussed their black-sheep son with writer Robert Goerman, who happened to be their neighbor. They showed Goerman letters in which Carl bragged about his role in creating a modern legend. Carl's brother, Randolph, told the writer that Carl had "a fantastic mind. But so far as I know, he's never really used it." Carl Allen is said to have died sometime in the 1980s.

DREAMLAND--A UFO HOLDING AREA
- - - -

A rea 51, located in a corner of the Nevada Test Site and sometimes called "Dreamland," is said to be the place where experts work on the secrets of UFO technology.

Nevada Test Site
Harbors Remains of Alien Spaceships!

On November 11 and 13, 1989, Las Vegas's KLAS-TV (an ABC affiliate) carried an astonishing story on its evening news show. The program—the outcome of a one and one-half year investigation by reporter George Knapp—focused on Robert Lazar, who claimed to have been employed at Area 51 in a location designated S-4. Lazar told Knapp that he had been hired by the navy to study some classified technical papers on advanced propulsion systems, and related that he was alarmed to read about systems that were far ahead of anything that could be based on conventional physics. "The power source," he said, "is an antimatter reactor."

Con Men Continued: Newton and GeBauer had stolen their hoax idea from another hoax involving a B-movie producer, Mikel Conrad, who claimed that a 1949 science-fiction film of his, *The Flying Saucer*, contained actual scenes of a spaceship in government custody. (Conrad had even hired an actor to pose as an FBI agent to swear that the story was true.) Inspired by the newspaper coverage of Conrad's show-business scam, Newton and GeBauer decided to dress up their oil swindle with a touch of UFO pizzazz.

Hangars full of alien discs. In due course, Lazar said, he was taken into a hangar where he saw a disc. Although he had been instructed to walk by the craft without looking directly at it, he touched the disc briefly as he passed by. He later saw the object in flight and was allowed to view eight other craft in connecting hangars that were separated by large bay doors. Each craft had a distinctive appearance, but all were disc-shaped.

Lazar's superiors told him nothing about the nature of these discs or about how they had been recovered. Managing to get a glimpse inside one, he saw that "it had really some [small] chairs"—as if the pilots of the craft were of shorter-than-human stature.

The story began to fall together "just all too fast." After having seen the discs in flight, Lazar was convinced that no earthly technology could be responsible for what he had seen. One thing in particular made him certain of his conclusion: He discovered that a substance unknown to earthly science, element 115, played a major role in the development of the gravity-harnessing technology.

A lack of credentials. During his investigation, Knapp interviewed a "technician in a highly sensitive position," who told him it was "common knowledge among those with high-security clearances that recovered alien discs are stored at the Nevada Test Site."

Lazar's story, however, proved to be somewhat of a mystery for the reporter: Unable to locate documentation to support Lazar's claims about his professional and educational background, Knapp admitted that "checking out Lazar's credentials proved to be a difficult task." Even polygraph tests didn't provide any answers. Nevertheless, Knapp thought that Lazar was probably telling the truth.

Lazar was, for a while, an international UFO celebrity. George Knapp put together a follow-up television special about his story, and he also had darksider John Lear on his side. However, his lack of supporting evidence and evasiveness about key issues caused even Lazar's staunchest supporters to doubt his wild claims about the Nevada Test Site. Nonetheless, Lazar has never confessed to making up the story about alien discs at Area 51.

A Secret Government? So-called "dark-siders" believe that a sinister "secret government" consisting of the Central Intelligence Agency (CIA), the National Security Agency, and the Council on Foreign Relations runs the United States and murders all those who get in their way including President John F. Kennedy, who threatened to blow the whistle on them. Dark-siders also believe that this evil American secret government operates in collaboration with the Trilateral Commission and the Bilderbergers, a Geneva-based international secret society.

GEORGE ADAMSKI
SPOTS VENUSIAN SPACECRAFT
- - - -

When a Venusian "scoutcraft" landed in a southern California desert on November 20, 1952, George Adamski—a well-known figure in occult circles—communicated with its occupant. Three weeks later, the low-flying scoutcraft passed over Adamski's residence, enabling him to take clear pictures of the alien aircraft. These were hardly Adamski's first flying saucer snapshots; he'd been taking them for the past three years.

Man Is Frequent Flyer on Alien Aircraft!

Adamski's account of his experiences was published in 1953 as part of a book titled *Flying Saucers Have Landed;* also included was a manuscript by Desmond Leslie that dealt with spaceships in ancient history and in mystical tradition. The book was extremely popular and influential. Three years after *Flying Saucers* was published, Adamski was listed as the author of *Inside the Space Ships* (ghostwritten by Charlotte Blodget). In it, Adamski described his frequent flights in flying saucers and meetings with Venusians, Martians, and Saturnians.

How to Hoax a Hoaxer: James W. Moseley and Gray Barker composed a letter to Adamski on State Department stationery. The letter, signed "R. E. Straith, Cultural Exchange Committee," informed Adamski that the "Department has on file a great deal of confirmatory evidence bearing out your own claims.... While certainly the Department cannot publicly confirm your experiences, it can, I believe with propriety, encourage your work." Although the State Department immediately denied knowing anything of either Straith or of his committee, Adamski told his followers that after a "thorough investigation" he had learned that both existed--but were highly classified.

In his book *Inside the Space Ships,* George Adamski described the saucer people he had met. Spiritually and physically beautiful, the "Space Brothers" meant to stop humans from destroying themselves with atomic weapons. Their "cosmic philosophy" was very similar to theosophy, the movement that holds that there is basic truth in all religions.

Most people—including ufologists—found Adamski's ideas absurd. But he did have followers who defended him energetically in books and newsletters. In May 1959, Adamski toured Europe and—despite the disapproval of the Dutch press, the scientific community, and university students (who interrupted one of his lectures with jeers and flying fruit)—he was granted an audi-

One of George Adamski's UFOtographs, allegedly taken December 13, 1952.

ence with Queen Juliana of The Netherlands. Later, however, even though he had met with Juliana, few people were inclined to believe him when he claimed to have been called to a secret conference with Pope John XXIII.

A fraud in the making. Adamski's harshest critics were ufologists who believed that the occultist's wild stories hurt their cause. James W. Moseley, the editor of *Saucer News,* dealt a blow to Adamski's reputation by publishing

an exposé that was based on interviews of people who had been around him during the eventful period in late 1952. One of Moseley's informants, Jerrold Baker, claimed to have seen the model that was used to fake the photographs of the Venusian spacecraft. He also claimed to have heard a tape recording of Adamski and associates rehearsing what they were going to tell the public about an upcoming alien "contact."

A twice-hoaxed tale. Moseley couldn't resist the temptation to hoax a hoaxer. He and a friend, Gray Barker, a UFO and contactee publisher, managed to get copies of State Department stationery, with the department seal impressed on the paper. Using the stationery, they wrote Adamski a letter—from "the Department"—to express their approval of his saucer flights and alien contacts. Adamski believed it; unaware of Moseley's involvement, he tried to get his analysis printed in Moseley's magazine. Moseley declined—and never confessed the hoax until January 1985, one month after his coconspirator Barker had died.

Lost face and wary followers. In 1962, Adamski's alien travels took him a little too far out: Many of his followers found it hard to believe that their leader had attended a meeting on Saturn. They were annoyed at his sudden involvement in psychic practices, an area he had always strenuously criticized. Adamski's reputation suffered another blow when one of his trusted associates, C. A. Honey, caught him in a scam to bilk gullible followers out of money. Adamski, it turned out, was running a for-profit operation on how to contact space people. Nevertheless—despite his supposed trips to Saturn and his designs to profit from space scams—Adamski had his followers, who believed that their leader had gone astray because he had fallen under evil extraterrestrial, demonic, or even CIA influence.

The Dark-Side Movement:

Where there are tales of aliens and UFOs, there are rumors of conspiracies and cover-ups. The "dark side hypothesis" spells out a sinister government plan: In order to deal with the alien menace without letting the rest of the human race know what was happening, America's secret government needed to raise vast sums of money quickly. It entered into the drug trade, putting a Texas oil company president, George Bush, in charge of the enterprise. In order to reduce the population, the secret government introduced deadly diseases including AIDS. Gun control laws form another aspect of the master plan: With laws to regulate access to guns, criminals (some of whom are trained by the CIA) would have free reign to terrorize law-abiding Americans. Meanwhile, in vast underground tunnels in the Southwest, evil human and alien scientists are tending enormous vats in which soulless android slaves are being created to replace human beings.

THE MAURY ISLAND HOAX: THE DIRTIEST HOAX IN UFO HISTORY

- - - -

In the summer of 1947, unidentified flying objects blasted into public consciousness. On June 24, Kenneth Arnold, a private pilot, sighted nine fast-moving disc-shaped objects streaking in formation over Mount Rainier, Washington. In an interview with a newspaper reporter, Arnold described the movement of the flying discs he had seen as saucers skipping over water. The term "flying saucers"—which has survived for almost fifty years—was coined by an anonymous headline writer. Although later proven to be a hoax, Arnold's report sparked a spate of similar sightings.

Witnesses Spot
Flying Donuts Near Maury Island!

About three weeks after his June 24 sighting, Arnold received word from Ray Palmer, a Chicago editor. Palmer's publications, two science-fiction magazines called *Amazing Stories* and *Fantastic Adventures,* regularly published material on "true mysteries"—which included what had suddenly become known as flying saucers.

Palmer wanted Arnold to write about what he had seen. In a follow-up letter, he casually asked Arnold if he would look into a story he had heard from one Fred L. Crisman, who claimed to have recovered pieces of a flying saucer. What Palmer didn't mention was that Crisman had approached him before with bizarre stories of alien encounters: Sometime earlier, in a letter, Crisman claimed to have been involved in a gunfight—in a cave—with hostile alien creatures.

Even though Arnold noticed that Palmer "didn't seem to be real cranked up" about the flying saucer story, he flew to Tacoma, Washington, to interview Crisman and Harold Dahl. Identifying himself as a harbor patrolman, Dahl said that on June 21, 1947, he, his son, and two crew members had seen six donut-shaped objects east of Maury Island. One, apparently in trouble, spewed out two kinds of metal—one white and light, the other dark and "similar to lava rock." He also said that he had filmed the objects.

The next day a mysterious stranger, who seemed to know everything about the incident, warned Dahl not to discuss it further. That didn't stop the patrolman from telling Crisman—supposedly his superior in the harbor patrol—who then went to the beach to collect samples. Later, when Arnold inspected one of the samples, he immediately recognized it as lava rock.

Interview with a hoaxer. Arnold was hooked. He contacted a new friend who had recently experienced a much-publicized sighting. United Air-

DONALD KEYHOE—HOW THE SAUCERS FLY

FATE
ANC
MAGAZINE

November 1954 35¢

BOAC's FLYING JELLYFISH

AIR CHIEF MARSHAL LORD DOWDING

"WHY I BELIEVE IN SAUCERS"

A November 1954 edition of the science fiction magazine *Fate*.

lines pilot E. J. Smith flew up the next day to help Arnold interview the two men. After the interview—which took place in their hotel room—Smith and Arnold received a mysterious phone call. A local reporter called to say that someone had called his office and had given a word-for-word report of their secret discussion. Smith and Arnold searched for microphones but found none.

The next morning Crisman and Dahl showed them samples of the lava rock and the white metal. Arnold believed the metal to be "ordinary aluminum which certain sections of all large military aircraft are made of." Slow to suspect a scam, Arnold's confidence was unshaken—even when Dahl said he had given the UFO film to Crisman, who claimed to have "misplaced" it.

Arnold decided that the story was far too big for him and Smith alone. He contacted Lieutenant Frank M. Brown, a military intelligence officer at Hamilton Field in California. Within two hours, Brown—who had investigated Arnold's sighting—flew to Washington, D.C., in a B-25, accompanied by Captain William L. Davidson. As soon as Brown and Davidson saw the fragments, they lost interest, excusing themselves as politely as they could without hurting Arnold's feelings or giving away their conclusions about the rock and metal fragments.

With no further ado, the two boarded their B-25 to return to California. Less than an hour later, the engine caught fire, and both officers died in the resulting crash. The so-called "mysterious" circumstances of the crash became the subject of flying saucer folklore: The two men had died, some believed, because they "knew too much about flying saucers."

The hoaxers confess. The follow-up air force investigation laid the hoax to rest. Crisman and Dahl—who had made the calls to the reporter's office—confessed that the story was a joke that had gotten out of hand. The air force never officially informed Arnold of its findings, and he continued to believe that the air force was covering up what it knew about the "Maury Island mystery."

In a memoir of his years at Project Blue Book, *The Report on Unidentified Flying Objects* (1956), Captain Edward J. Ruppelt called the affair the "dirtiest hoax in UFO history." Hoaxes comprised only slightly more than 1 percent of the reports in the air force's Project Blue Book files, and many of these involved photographs.

OTIS CARR'S FOURTH DIMENSIONAL SPACE VEHICLE

- - - -

I have invented a fourth dimensional space vehicle," New York hotel clerk Otis T. Carr announced in 1957. Shaped like a flying saucer, Carr's vehicle was powered by a revolutionary "Utron Electric Accumulator ... operating in unison with the free energy of the universe." The young clerk, who had befriended the elderly electrical scientist Nikola Tesla, claimed to be knowledgeable about the scientist's many secrets—secrets for which Tesla consid-

ered the human race unprepared. Carr, on the other hand, was prepared to reveal the astonishing secrets he had learned ... for a price.

New York Hotel Clerk
Shoots for the Moon and Lands in Jail!

Carr set up OTC Enterprises in Baltimore, Maryland, in 1955 and secured funding from a prominent businessman in the city. He also hired Norman Evans Colton, a skilled promotion man who sent out a slew of "information bulletins" to investors and other people interested in OTC's projects. The bulletins "explained" the mechanics of flying saucers in clear and easy-to-understand sentences such as these:

Mount this whole rotating body, with its spindle, on another platform and rotate this platform on a spindle[;] then, if the counter-rotation is greater than the initial forward rotation of the body, a dip-needle on the second platform will point down while the first dip-needle points up, indicating the complete relativity of the polarity. When the exact counter-rotation matches the forward rotation, the body loses its polarity entirely and immediately becomes activated by free-energy (tensor stresses in space) and acts as an independent force.

Extraterrestrials and Ice Cream:

Rumors of government-extraterrestrial contacts led to an interesting moment on national TV. In 1949, an alien being supposedly survived a crash and was housed at Los Alamos, New Mexico, until it died of unknown causes in 1952. Some people believed that the incident was part of a series of government conspiracies and cover-ups involving aliens and UFOs. Two alleged cover-up insiders, "Falcon" and "Condor," told their stories on a nationally syndicated television show. With their faces shaded and voices altered, they announced a startling revelation on "UFO Cover-up ... Live": Extraterrestrials like strawberry ice cream!

Surprisingly, Carr managed to capture respectful press attention as he discussed his plans to construct a spaceship. The price tag for the OTC-X1—a craft forty-five feet in diameter and fifteen feet high—was to be a whopping $20 million.

OTC Enterprises relocated to Oklahoma City, Oklahoma, where Carr had found some particularly enthusiastic and well-heeled investors. There, he announced his plans for the OTC-X1: On December 7, 1959, he would pilot the spacecraft from the earth to the moon and back. (This was an impressive promise at the time: *Apollo 8*, the first U.S. flight to the moon, would not lift off until December 21, 1968.) Meanwhile, on Sunday, April 19, a six-foot test model would launch its first flight from an Oklahoma City amusement park at three o'clock in the afternoon.

A greater scientist than Einstein. Investors assumed that Otis Carr and his public relations man, Norman Evans Colton, knew what they were doing; the duo garnered thousands of dollars in spite of their frequent public blunders. On Long John Nebel's WOR radio show in June 1958, Carr remarked that he could not "even begin to enumerate" the discoveries of Nikola Tesla, the brilliant scientist who was supposed to have been his teacher. Skeptical, a fellow guest asked him to "enumerate just one or two of them," but Carr could only mutter, "That's funny—I cannot remember even one." It seems Carr, who declared himself a greater scientist than Albert Einstein, could not recite even one of Isaac Newton's three laws of motion. Memorizing such things, publicity-man Colton hastily explained, was "a waste of time."

Moon trip leads to jail. Despite the hordes of journalists, curiosity-seekers, and contactees (one of whom swore that "Captain Karnu" and his five invisible spaceships were monitoring the situation), the test was delayed for three days. The test model, it seems, had sprung a "mercury leak." Carr, in the meantime, had come down with a sudden throat ailment, and was conveniently confined to an area hospital.

Three days later the test was called off entirely. Nebel, who had flown down from his New York radio station, demanded to be allowed into the factory where the OTC-X1 was stored. What he saw bore no particular resemblance to an aircraft: He caught a brief glimpse of what looked like a jumble of unconnected parts and wires. Shortly thereafter, a mysterious fire consumed the miscellaneous parts that Nebel had seen.

On May 4, in the county courthouse in Oklahoma City, questioned about stock sales to three wealthy local businessmen, Carr repeatedly took the fifth amendment. Two weeks later, Carr, Colton, and two OTC Enterprises salesmen were charged with illegal stock sales. Although Colton had fled the state and was unfindable, Carr was fined $5,000 for a single charge. Since the once-mighty OTC Enterprises had only $1.71 left in its checking account, he was sent to jail to work off the fine at a dollar a day. Carr, who eventually faded from the public eye, died years later in a Pittsburgh, Pennsylvania slum.

A persistent con man. Colton attempted to revive OTC Enterprises— until the New York state attorney general stepped in to stop him. Undaunted, he created the Millennium Agency and sought out customers for "free energy machines ... operated entirely by environmental gravitic forces" which would "draw electricity from the atmosphere without the use of any fuel." Apparently, no one was interested.

Saints, Spirits
and Supernatural
Scams

FAITH HEALING

- - - -

The human body sometimes seems to heal itself spontaneously, and a number of hoaxers have counted on the fact that people simply don't know it happens. Faith healers claim to be able to heal the ill and the disabled through special powers given to them by God. Whether there really is such a thing as a genuine faith healer, one thing is sure: It's much easier to discover a hoax than it is to prove the real thing.

Faith Healers Work Miracles Thanks to "Dr. Jesus"!

When James Randi, a magician and exposer of frauds, and others decided to investigate faith healers in 1985 and 1986, they limited their study to those who appeared to be employing some form of mentalism. In other words, they targeted faith healers who used the same sorts of "mind reading" tricks that magicians use in magic acts.

On the revival circuit, faith healing is known as "calling out"; in other circles, it's known as a mentalist's routine. The faith healer approaches a person in the audience by name—even though there is no way the healer supposedly could have known the name—and announces the medical problems that afflict that person. The healer often adds personal details—thanks, supposedly, to communicating with God or Dr. Jesus—such as the person's address and the names of doctors who have treated the condition.

Investigation targets phony faith healers. W. V. Grant was one of the best known faith healers to employ calling out. He and Peter Popoff, another healer who employed this technique, were the main focus of the investigation conducted by the Committee for the Scientific Examination of Religion (with the assistance of James Randi).

The investigation of Grant produced a number of details about his life and his healing methods. Grant claims to have been a star football player in high school, and to have received seventy-seven National Collegiate Ath-

letic Association (NCAA) football scholarship offers; Grant's coach, however, says he didn't receive a single scholarship offer. Grant also claims to have gone to the University of California, Los Angeles, but UCLA has no record of him. As for the doctor of divinity he claims to have received from "Midstates Bible College" in Iowa, it sounds impressive, but no one—including the Iowa Department of Public Instruction, the American Association of Bible Colleges, and the Association of Theological Schools—has any record of the school's existence.

The committee decided to conduct a follow-up investigation of a man who had been cured, according to Grant, by "closed-heart surgery" performed by Dr. Jesus. Six physicians—all named by Grant—had supposedly scheduled this man for open-heart surgery in Georgia, but the investigation found none of these six doctors on the register of Georgia physicians. One of the hospitals mentioned had no record of the patient; what's more, the hospital *never* performed open-heart surgery.

The committee also discovered that a number of people who had been healed by Grant were no better off after Grant had pronounced them "cured." One individual still had a blind eye, another was still totally blind, and yet another continued to suffer from diabetes—but that didn't stop Grant from using pictures of them in his magazine as proof of his power as a miracle healer.

The old wheelchair trick. At each of Grant's services, a number of people sat in the front in wheelchairs. When Grant pronounced them healed, they were able to rise out of their chairs. This didn't require much of a miracle: These people had arrived on their own two feet. Grant's organization—which supplied most of the wheelchairs—asked people who *walked* into the auditorium, but who were in need of some type of healing, to sit in the wheelchairs. These wheelchairs were then pushed to the front of the auditorium. People who came in their *own* wheelchairs (and presumably needed them), were wheeled to the rear of the auditorium; Grant somehow managed to overlook those who *arrived* in wheelchairs.

The committee looked into the practice of calling out at Grant's rallies. They found that if people went early, they were assured of an aisle seat where Grant could talk to them during the service; this drew a lot of early arrivals.

James Randi Puts Faith Healers to the Test: In his book *The Faith Healers*, Randi lists five requirements that must be met to prove that a faith healing is genuine: 1.) The disease involved must not normally cure itself after a given period of time; 2.) The recovery must be complete; 3) The recovery must take place in the absence of any medical treatment that might normally be expected to affect the disease; 4.) There must be adequate medical opinion that the disease was present *before* the miracle took place; and 5.) There must be adequate medical opinion to verify that the disease is not present *after* the healing has taken place.

Dressed casually, Grant asked these people questions—finding out their names, the names of their physicians, and their illnesses, so he could decide whom to "heal" during the service.

Grant also instructed everyone on his mailing list to come early, and to hand their "special offering envelopes" to him personally. As each person came up to the stage to hand Grant his or her envelope—with his or her name written on the front—the wily preacher would stare at them intently for a second or two. This, Randi realized, was no small show of sincerity: Grant was committing each person's name and face to memory.

After receiving the envelopes, Grant retired backstage. There, he opened the envelopes and read each person's "healing cards" in private, memorizing personal details to go with the faces he had committed to memory. Grant may not have been a healer, but he must have had a phenomenal memory—and the notes he concealed in his Bible helped to jog his recollection.

James Randi got hold of some of Grant's crib sheets that had been thrown into the trash after one of the services. He also found letters from those who had been "healed," outlining the details of their illnesses. One of the crib sheets said this: "Anthony—deaf in both ears, and bladder and tumors. Connie—pain in left eye and left jaw, thyroid and arthritis. Digestive problems. Bernadette—psoriasis, arthritis. Michael—deaf in left ear. Syl—high blood pressure."

The bug in Peter Popoff's ear. The committee also investigated faith healer Peter Popoff, and what they found alarmed them. Popoff did not associate with his audience before the service. He worked with no crib notes, yet he was able to conduct a smooth "calling out" performance. He seemed to know—without any sort of prior information—people's names and illnesses, and the names of their physicians. He looked like the real thing.

Silver-Screen Faith Healing: The 1992 movie *Leap of Faith*, starring Steve Martin, is loosely based on what the committee found about Peter Popoff.

Then one of the committee members managed to get a close look at Popoff during a service: The "healer" wore a tiny hearing aid in his ear. It seems Popoff wasn't exactly hard of hearing. At a later service, an electronics whiz working for the committee managed to sneak an electronic scanner into the auditorium. A search of the frequencies in use in the immediate area soon located a transmitter on 39.17 megahertz that was carrying the voice of Popoff's wife directly into the minister's ear. Backstage, reading from the "prayer cards," she transmitted information about the various audience members. The committee recorded the transmissions from Elizabeth to Popoff, and Randi later played some of them on *The Tonight Show* with Johnny Carson. Popoff's public was not amused; many TV stations later canceled his services, and the phoney faith healer eventually declared bankruptcy. He did, however, stage a comeback—presumably with no form of hearing enhancement.

POPE JOAN

– – – –

Some people say that the Pope known as John VIII was really a woman. John VIII—who was supposedly in office for two years, five months, and four days, between the years 853 and 855—was probably known as John Anglicus (English John) before becoming pope.

Pope John VIII
Was Really a Woman in Disguise!

Though a few sources cite some general references to Pope Joan before the thirteenth century, the first significant reference to her dates to the mid-thirteenth century, about 350 years after she was supposed to have reigned. The *Chronicle of Metz* provides some telling details about the life of the "popess":

Desperately Seeking Pope Joan:

Author Robert Ware provides many excerpts from Catholic sources that not only mention but give descriptive information about Pope Joan. He lists forty-five sources from before the year 1500, dating from as early as 937. Most importantly, six of them are from before the middle of the thirteenth century (1250)--the date when, according to modern Catholic authorities, Pope Joan is first mentioned in any detail.

Query: With regard to a certain pope—or rather popess, because she was a woman who pretended to be a man. By his excellent abilities having been appointed notary at the papal court he became Cardinal and eventually Pope. On a certain day, when he was riding, he gave birth to a child, and straightaway in accordance with Roman justice his feet were tied together and he was dragged for half a league at a horse's tail while the people stoned him. At the place where he expired, he was buried, and an inscription was set up: PETRE PATER PATRUM PAPISSE PODITO PARTUM. [This Peter, the father of fathers, gave birth to a child.] Under him was instituted the fast of the Ember Days, and it is called the popess's fast.

More evidence of a woman pope. The next reference to Pope Joan occurs about fifty years later, in a work called the *Chronicon Pontificum et Imperatorum (Chronicle of Popes and Emperors),* by Martinus Polonus (who was also known as Martin of Troppau). It says:

After the aforesaid Leo, John, an Englishman by descent, who came from Mainz, held the see two years, five months and four days, and the pontificate was vacant one month. He died at Rome. He, it is asserted, was a woman. And having been taken by her lover to Athens in man's clothes, she made such progress in various sciences that there was nobody equal to her. So that afterwards lecturing on the Trivium at Rome she had great masters for her disciples and hearers. And forasmuch as she was in great esteem in the city, both for her life and her learning, she was unanimously elected pope. But while pope she became pregnant by the person with whom she was intimate. But not knowing the time of her delivery, while going from St. Peter's to the Lateran, being taken in labor, she brought forth a child between the Coliseum and St. Clement's church. And afterwards dying she was, it is said, buried in that place. And because Lord Pope always turns aside from that way, there are some who are fully persuaded that it is done in detestation of the fact. Nor is she put in the Catalogue of the Holy Popes, as well on account of her female sex as on account of the shameful nature of the episode.

A depiction of Pope Joan giving birth.

Pope Joan, according to Martin of Troppau, was not included in the list of Holy Popes because she had sinned *and* because she was a woman.

Old coins tell a different story. A man by the name of Horace Mann believes that there was no woman pope known as Pope Joan. He points out that there are coins that picture Pope Benedict III and the emperor Lothaire together on the same coin. Pope Leo I—who was pope before Benedict—died on July 17, 855, while Lothaire died on September 28, 855. A little math makes one thing clear: If Benedict and Lothaire reigned at the same time—as the coin suggests—it must have been during the period between July 17 and September 28, 855. That leaves Joan out in the cold: There was no period between 853 and 855 when she could have been pope. Some people speculate, however, that the date of Leo's death was later changed from 853 to 855, which brings us back to the possibility that a woman donned the pope's robes between 853 and 855.

The Church responds. The Roman Catholic Church's response to the Pope Joan question has changed over the years. At first, the church seemed to accept the woman pope as real. After the Reformation in the sixteenth century, however, the church began to deny the existence of a woman pope named Joan.

Vials of Tears and Crowns of Thorns:

Over the centuries, phoney religious relics have been commonplace. The Shroud of Turin is hardly an original: Some forty cloths have been identified as the holy shroud. Fourteen nails have been identified as the nails that fastened Jesus to the cross, when only three or four were supposedly used. Adding to the list of fake relics are vials of Jesus' tears and his mother's milk, countless pieces of the True Cross, and thorns from the Crown of Thorns.

Whether or not Joan was pope, somebody somewhere instigated a hoax. If the woman was indeed a pope, then members of the church have confused the issue. If she were not pope, then somewhere among the people who believe in the woman pope there lives a hoaxer.

THE SHROUD OF TURIN

- - - -

The four apostles of the New Testament recorded the existence of a linen cloth used at the burial of Christ after his crucifixion. Many people believe that the Shroud of Turin is that same burial cloth. A number of scientific tests, however, have proven the holy shroud to be a medieval hoax and forgery.

A close-up of the face of Christ as it appears in the Shroud of Turin.

Burial Shroud Is
Photographic Negative of Crucified Christ!

The cloth—a fourteen-foot sheet of linen that seems to bear the imprints of a crucified man—was first mentioned in about 570 by a pilgrim who said it was kept in a monastery by the river Jordan. About 100 years later, the French

Bishop Arculph was shipwrecked on the coast of Scotland and traveled to a monastery on the island of Iona. Here he said he saw the shroud and actually kissed it. More references to the Shroud appear intermittently until the mid-fourteenth century when it turned up in a small wooden church in Lirey, France. Geoffrey de Charny, a soldier of fortune, owned the cloth, but was either unable or unwilling to say how he had acquired the fabulous "relic."

Soon after the cloth appeared at Lirey, a scandal ensued. A report written to Pope Clement in 1389 revealed that the "shroud" was being used to bilk money out of unsuspecting miracle-seekers. Exhibited by the dean of a church at Lirey, the Holy Shroud was being used "to attract the multitude so that money might cunningly be wrung from them." The report further explained that "pretended miracles were worked, certain men being hired to represent themselves as healed at the moment of the exhibition of the Shroud."

Eventually, a bishop "discovered the fraud and how the said cloth had been cunningly painted, the truth being attested by the artist who had painted it." This was all Pope Clement needed to hear. Calling the cloth a painted representation, he forbade anyone to display it as the genuine article.

The shroud is sold. In 1453, after a century of scandal, Geoffrey de Charny's granddaughter, Margaret, got hold of the shroud. After touring with the "relic," she eventually sold it to the Duke of Savoy. Sometimes portrayed as a religious woman who "gave" the shroud to the duke, Margaret was in turn blessed with the price of a castle and the revenues of an estate. The church was not so generous and, frowning on Margaret's initiative, excommunicated her. This apparently bothered Margaret not the least, and she died in 1460.

The Duke of Savoy's family—which later became the Italian monarchy—exhibited the cloth, claiming that it was the Holy Shroud which possessed magical protective powers. Magical powers or not, in 1532 the cloth had to be rescued from a fire that destroyed the chapel where it was displayed. A bit of molten silver—from the box in which the shroud was kept—penetrated the cloth's many folds, creating the burn marks and patches that surround the image on the shroud.

Evidence of forgery. When the image on the shroud was first photographed in 1898, the dark and light spots were reversed. People who believed the shroud was real compared the image to a photographic negative, calling it a miraculous "photo" of Jesus. Actually, the image is only approximately negative, since the hair and beard are both positive. The negative impression can be duplicated, it turns out, by taking a rubbing from a bas-relief.

Better photographs of the shroud became available in the 1930s. A number of shroud supporters insisted that certain aspects of the image were beyond the knowledge and abilities of a medieval forger. Others disagreed, noting that the footprint on the cloth did not match the image of the leg that

belonged to it. And a number of other details didn't add up: The features of the body were unnaturally elongated (strangely similar to figures portrayed in French Gothic art of roughly the same period). The hair fell as if the figure were upright, rather than lying down. And the "blood"—which failed to mat the hair—remained red, unlike old blood, which blackens over time.

From 1969 to 1976, an official committee carried out physical tests of the shroud. When the press found out about the commission—whose members had started out in secret—church authorities of Turin, Italy, denied its existence. Forced to admit that the commission *did* exist, the Turin authorities limited the availability of the commission's report, which questioned the origin of the cloth and suggested that the shroud was an artistic work made by some imprinting technique. The church's counter response, on the other hand, was available to anyone who showed interest.

The shroud fails a blood test. Two forensic serologists put the "blood"-stained threads through extensive tests. The blood failed all of them. The experts tested for hemoglobin, conducted microscopic examinations to look for blood corpuscles, and performed other analyses using highly technical instruments. What they found didn't look like blood: They reported the presence of a reddish granule that would not dissolve when they tried to analyze it. Yet another expert found what others had suspected all along: He discovered what looked like traces of paint.

In 1978, the Shroud of Turin Research Project (STURP) continued to examine the cloth. Many of the project members, however, had already made up their minds about the shroud's authenticity. STURP's leaders, it seems, served on the Catholic Holy Shroud Guild, whose members staunchly defended the holy shroud as a genuine relic. Other STURP scientists revealed that they leaned in favor of the authenticity of the shroud *before they ever examined the shroud.* And the project was hardly an assembly of experts: All but one of the STURP scientists lacked expertise in identifying paint pigments and in detecting art forgeries.

More Questionable Relics: Sometime around 620, in Thrace, the clothing of the Virgin Mary was "discovered" with no explanation. Pope Gregory (who reigned from 996 to 999) said that he had found Mary's wedding ring in Italy. It didn't seem to matter to him that in the first century, Jewish people did not wear wedding rings. Many churches also had articles of Mary's clothing including her girdles--among their relics. Other such "found" religious "relics" include the plate on which the lamb was served at the last supper; the stone on which Mohammed (or Jesus, or Mary) stood while ascending to heaven; the blood of Jesus; letters from Jesus (now lost); clothing of Jesus; portraits of the apostles; and pieces of wood from Noah's Ark.

The Shroud of Turin is to some a holy relic, to others, a hoax.

The one exception was Walter McCrone, an internationally famous micro-analyst. He performed "blind" studies of samples taken from the shroud, and found significant amounts of the pigment red ocher (red iron oxide) on image areas; he didn't, however, find any pigment on the cloth where there was no image. The blood on the shroud, McCrone found, was nothing more than tempera paint containing red ocher and another pigment, vermillion.

STURP refused to endorse McCrone's report, and held him to a legal agreement not to reveal his results. However, when this "covenant not to disclose" expired, he published his reports, which exposed the spurious paint globules and pigment particles.

The "experts" lack experience. McCrone—who claims to have been "drummed out" of STURP—was replaced by John Heller and Alan Adler. The two scientists soon claimed that McCrone's findings and those of the commission scientists were inaccurate. They also claimed that they had "identified" the presence of blood on the shroud. It seemed, at first, that Heller and Adler might have discovered something that McCrone had overlooked. But it was their credentials that had been overlooked: Neither scientist was an expert in blood or pigment analysis. Heller admitted that McCrone "had over two decades of experience with this kind of problem and a worldwide reputation." He and Adler, on the other hand, "had never before tackled anything remotely like an artistic forgery."

Another expert by the name of John F. Fischer reviewed Heller and Adler's claims. He found that none of their tests was specific for blood, and that their approach to identifying blood was not scientifically acceptable. In fact, Heller and Adler could have obtained the same results from tempera paint.

In a presentation to the International Association for Identification (an organization of police officials and individuals engaged in forensic sciences, investigation, and scientific crime detection work), Fischer also noted that analysis of the blood produced results that were fundamentally inconsistent with genuine blood.

Three laboratories—in England, Switzerland, and Arizona—used radiocarbon tests to date the shroud. Performing analyses on small swatches cut from the cloth, the three labs produced dates that were surprisingly close. They determined that the cloth had been produced sometime between 1260 and 1390, a time span that coincides with the forger's confession.

PROTOCOLS OF THE ELDERS OF ZION

- - - -

T he *Protocols of the Elders of Zion* started out as a nineteenth-century political satire. Reinterpreted as an anti-Semitic tract, it was eventually adopted as Nazi propaganda.

Fake Document Fuels Nazi Furnace!

The *Protocols* has a tangled and mysterious history. Although we don't know exactly how the *Protocols* developed, it appears that the episode began

in Paris, France, in 1864. In that year, a political satirist named Maurice Joly published his book *A Dialog in Hell between Montesquieu and Machiavelli (Dialogue aux Enfer entre Montesquieu et Machiavel)*. Although the book was actually published in Brussels, Belgium, its title page said it was published in Geneva, Switzerland.

Joly's *Dialog* openly criticized Emperor Napoleon III—a criminal offense at the time—by putting the emperor's words in the mouths of Machiavelli and Montesquieu, two political philosophers whose theories were out of favor with Napoleon III's government. The book was smuggled into France, but was seized at the border. Arrested and tried, Joly was sentenced to fifteen months imprisonment on April 25, 1865.

Dog-eared Dialog: The Bibliotheque Nationale in France houses a copy of Joly's *Dialog*. The book has markings that indicate that it was probably the copy used to provide information for the *Protocols*.

After Joly's *Dialog* was banned and copies were confiscated, the book soon became a rare work. The work's obscurity would later help to hide the fact that the *Protocols* actually lifted large sections of the imaginary dialog from the satirical, and fictional, French work.

In Berlin, in 1868, Hermann Goedsche, a minor official in the German Postal Service (who wrote under the name of Sir John Retcliffe), published a novel called *Biarritz*. One chapter, called "In the Jewish Cemetery in Prague,"

The *Protocols* was published in America in 1920. That year, a Michigan newspaper belonging to Henry Ford (shown here), the *Dearborn Independent*, published a long series of articles defending the authenticity of the *Protocols*. These articles were published as a book, *The International Jew*, which Nazi leader Adolf Hitler later had translated and circulated throughout Germany.

describes a secret nighttime meeting held in the cemetery during the Feast of Tabernacles. There the leaders of the twelve tribes of Israel meet with the Devil to report on their activities during the century that has passed since their last meeting.

During the supposed meeting, the leaders report that the Jewish people are making great strides toward taking over the world. By exploiting the stock exchange, they have forced all the princes and governments of Europe into their debt. They discuss a scheme to put all lands under Jewish control, and outline plans to upset the Christian Church; they also talk about gaining control of the press, and discuss schemes to land high governmental positions. In short, their quest for world domination is going well. After renewing their oath, the leaders agree to meet again in 100 years.

A completely fictional work, *Biarritz* played on many of the fears that anti-Semites had voiced for hundreds of years.

A Russian conspirator. Pyotr Rachkovsky was the head of the foreign branch of the Russian secret police from 1884 to 1902. He organized the overseas operations of the Okhrana (secret police) in Paris (the overseas headquarters); Switzerland; London, England; and Berlin. Rachkovsky was also in charge of transforming the two fictional works by Joly and Goedsche into the *Protocols*.

In 1887, Rachkovsky planted a forged letter in the French press; it claimed the majority of terrorists active in France at that time were Jewish. Five years later, in Paris, Rachkovsy published a book titled *Anarchie et Nihilisme,* which claimed that the French Revolution made the Jew "the absolute master of the situation in Europe ... governing by discreet means both monarchies and republics." According to Rachkovsky's book, only one thing—the Jewish domination of Russia—had not yet been established; and this, the author argued, was already underway.

The book encouraged readers to form a Franco-Russian league to combat the powers of the Jewish people. Rachkovsky attempted to create such a league in 1902; although he failed, he later succeeded in creating the Union of the Russian People. Founded in 1905, the union conducted anti-Jewish activities, which included helping to circulate the *Protocols.*

In 1902, Rachkovsky was involved in a court intrigue with Sergey Nilus in St. Petersburg, Russia. A former landowner, Nilus had lost his entire fortune while living in France. After wandering in Russia from one monastery to another, he published a book in 1900. Nilus's book, *The Great in the Small,* explained how he had converted from an atheist to an Orthodox Christian.

Translations of the *Protocols*:

Translations of the *Protocols* began to circulate in Europe around 1919. Publication in Germany began in 1920 (although the earliest title page is dated 1919), and sales quickly reached 120,000 copies. The 1922 assassination of German Foreign Minister Walther Rathenau was motivated by the idea that Rathenau, a Jew, was one of the "Elders of Zion." An English translation, called *The Jewish Peril,* was published in 1920 by Eyre & Spottiswoode, publishers of the authorized version of the Bible and Anglican Prayer Book. Most reviewers accepted the work as authentic, although the newspapers published letters from readers who disagreed.

Nazi leader Adolf Hitler believed the *Protocols of the Elders of Zion* to be part of a Jewish conspiracy to destroy the Aryan race.

"Evidence" of a worldwide conspiracy. Somehow, Nilus obtained a copy of the *Protocols;* many believe that Rachkovsky sent him a copy, perhaps to continue their St. Petersburg court intrigue. When Nilus published a second edition of *The Great in the Small* in 1905, he included the *Protocols* as documentary "evidence" of a worldwide Jewish conspiracy. It seems Nilus believed that the world was in the throes of a Jewish takeover.

Once Nilus's version of the *Protocols* was published in 1905, the work took on a life of its own. Czar Nicholas II read and accepted the *Protocols*—which had been widely circulated in right-wing circles in Russia—as genuine. Once an investigation demonstrated that the work was a fraud, however, Nicholas refused to continue to allow the *Protocols* to be used as anti-Semitic propaganda.

The situation changed when the Czar was overthrown in the Russian Revolution. The "White" army, which had lost to the "Red" army, blamed the revolution on the Jews. The *Protocols* was widely read by the members of the "White" army, who believed that the work explained why and how the Jews were attempting to take over the world. This was the beginning of the myth of the Jewish-Communist conspiracy that helped to fuel the German campaign of anti-Semitism.

German nationalists and the "Jewish World Conspiracy." Beginning in 1920, the German National People's Party (DNVP) used racist propaganda—including the *Protocols*—in election campaigns. These campaigns focused on the "Jewish World Conspiracy"—a Jewish plot to destroy the Aryan race. Fueled by the German nationalist tradition (the "volkisch-racist"), the *Protocols* reinforced the anti-Semitic attitudes that led to the Holocaust.

The *Protocols* become a Nazi tool. Alfred Rosenberg, a writer who promoted Nazi anti-Semitism, was apparently influenced by the *Protocols* when he wrote *Myth of the Twentieth Century,* a book that came to be known as the sourcebook of Nazism. Hitler looked to the *Protocols* for an explanation of the tremendous economic inflation of 1923: "According to the *Protocols of Zion*," Hitler claimed, "the peoples are to be reduced to submission by hunger. The second revolution under the Star of David is the aim of the Jews in our time." The *Protocols*—which had started out as a hoax, probably for Russian political reasons—would later come to be known as a "warrant for genocide."

***Protocols* Tied to the Dreyfus Affair:** Author Norman Cohn is "practically certain" that the *Protocols* was made up in Paris sometime between 1894 and 1899. That corresponds with the time of the Dreyfus Affair, an anti-Semitic incident in which a Jewish army captain was accused of treason.

BRIDEY MURPHY AND PAST LIVES

---- - ----

The Search for Bridey Murphy, by Morey Bernstein, was a best-seller in 1956. Bernstein, an amateur hypnotist, uncovered Bridey Murphy, an Irish woman from the early nineteenth century, quite by accident. Using hypnosis, he "regressed" a woman he called Ruth Simmons backwards in time; so far back in time, in fact, that she remembered a previous life.

Nineteenth-Century Irish Woman Returns to World of Living!

The Bridey Murphy case was hardly the first time that a person had been regressed past birth under hypnosis. But, publicity, in the form of newspaper coverage and a best-selling novel, set this story apart from the others. The public was quick to believe a tale that suggested it was possible to survive death. When *Denver Post* reporter William J. Barker wrote several articles about the story for his newspaper's Sunday magazine section, Bridey Murphy took her place in history.

Doubleday publishing company eventually offered Bernstein a book contract, and the story of Bridey Murphy hit the best-seller list. At the same time, the *Chicago Daily News* obtained the rights to republish parts of the book; this inspired the paper's arch rival, the *Chicago American,* to assign reporters to look for holes in the story. After discovering that Ruth Simmons—whose real name was Virginia Tighe—had spent much of her youth in Chicago, Illinois, the investigators came across a number of interesting details about the woman who had been hypnotized in Pueblo, Colorado.

Memories of a past life. When Bernstein asked Virginia Tighe to remember what had happened to her before birth, she volunteered a wealth of memories. This was the story of Bridey Murphy: Born in 1798 in Cork, Ireland, Bridget (Bridey) Kathleen Murphy was the daughter of Kathleen and Duncan Murphy, a Protestant barrister. Bridey lived with

Thirteen-year-old Virginia Tighe (Bridey Murphy) shoots the breeze with a neighbor.

her family, which included a brother, Duncan Blaine Murphy, just outside of Cork, in an area she called "The Meadows." Under hypnosis, Bridey remembered being punished for scratching the paint off of her metal bed when she was about four years old; she also remembered being read to as a child from two books, *The Green Bay* and another about the sorrow of Dierdre.

At the age of twenty, Bridey married Sean Brian Joseph MacCarthy, the son of another Cork barrister. Since MacCarthy's family was Catholic, they had two wedding ceremonies, one Protestant and one Catholic, performed by Father Joseph John Gorman at St. Theresa's Church in Belfast. Bridey and Sean made their home in a cottage on Dooley Road in Belfast.

Bridey's brother married Aimee Strayne, the daughter of Bridey's school mistress. The couple stayed in Cork and had children; Bridey and her husband, on the other hand, had no children. Sean, a barrister who taught at the law school at Queen's University in Belfast, also wrote about the law in the *Belfast News-Letter.* Bridey died in 1864 at the age of sixty-six.

The facts are investigated. Some of the facts in Tighe's story could be proved—or disproved. The *Denver Post* sent William Barker over to Ireland for three weeks to check out the story. Barker—who was not an experienced genealogist and had little experience with historical research—found little to contradict Bridey's story. But he didn't find much to support it, either. What Barker didn't realize was that Bridey's story was weakened by the fact that he did not find her husband's name on the lists of barristers: The lists at that time were both complete and accurate. Barker nonetheless had an idea why Bridey's husband's name was absent from the lists: Bridey exaggerated and had probably "remembered" a more glamorous profession for her bookkeeper husband.

***Life* calls Bridey's story "Hypnotizzy."** The *Chicago American*'s investigators were not so inclined to believe that Virginia Tighe was remembering her 100-year-old past. Tighe, it turns out, had an aunt who was born in Ireland. As a child in Chicago, she had listened to her aunt's many stories of her own childhood in the land of Erin. Across the street from young Virginia lived another Irish woman, who also told her stories about Ireland; the woman's name was Bridie Murphy Corkell. *Life* magazine soon got wind of these findings, and published the news as the "solution" to the Bridey Murphy mystery.

Flaws in Virginia Tighe's Story:

Tighe claimed to remember her life as a nineteenth-century Irish woman, yet there were some gaping holes in her memory. For instance, she was unable to speak any Gaelic, and she could not remember where she was buried, although she said she had witnessed her own funeral. She was also unable to offer information that fit with atlases and directories of the time. Publications showed no St. Theresa's Church, Dooley Road, or Mrs. Strayne's Day School. There is no evidence of a MacCarthy family of barristers or of a Father Joseph John Gorman. There is no indication that there were metal beds in Ireland in 1802, and no one has located a book from that time called *The Green Bay.*

William Barker responded to statements made by the *Chicago American* and *Life* by adding a chapter to the paperback edition of Bernstein's book. In it, he described some findings that supported Bridey's story. For example, Virginia Tighe had mentioned the names of two grocers, Carrigan and Farr; it's very difficult to explain how a woman who grew up in Chicago in the twentieth century would have known the names of two relatively unknown grocers who conducted business in Belfast for a few years in the mid-1800s.

Speak, Memory! Studies have demonstrated that a person can remember foreign languages heard in childhood even without understanding the language. An individual can repeat perfect sentences even though he or she does not consciously remember hearing or speaking the language before. The mind can also remember historical facts that have been lost to the conscious memory.

Borrowed memories. Was Virginia Tighe the reincarnation of a nineteenth-century Irish woman, or was Bridey Murphy the woman who never was? It's possible that Tighe's memory was playing tricks on her: Bridey's "recollections" may be nothing more than Tighe's forgotten memories of childhood stories. The entire episode might be a case of a hypnotized person trying to please the hypnotist. Or Bridey Murphy might have crossed the Atlantic—and then some—to pay the world a second visit.

HARRY HOUDINI ATTEMPTS TO COMMUNICATE WITH THE DEAD
- - - -

E hrich Weiss, born in 1874, was better known as the celebrated magician Harry Houdini. Close to his mother, he was shaken when she died in 1913. He decided to find out whether there was any truth to the idea that the spirit of his dead mother could communicate with him through a spiritualist medium; it didn't take long for Houdini, an expert on magic and sleight of hand, to find that mediumship was full of fakery.

Houdini Breaks Silence of Grave!

A number of mediums attempted to convince Houdini that his mother's spirit was talking to him. What they didn't realize was that Houdini's mother spoke no English and always called him "Ehrich." Angered by his discovery that mediums preyed on a public that did not easily see through magic tricks, Houdini began a crusade to challenge and expose bogus mediums. As a result, people began to regard mediums with suspicion.

Magician plans his escape from the spirit world. Despite his disappointment in trying to contact the spirit of his mother, Houdini wasn't going to rule out the possibility of communicating with the living after he died. He arranged with his wife Bess to use a code that would show he was trying to contact her. The code was based on a stage magic act they had performed together, and there was little chance of anyone else knowing the routine at the time of Houdini's unexpected death on Halloween in 1926.

For several years, Bess Houdini attended seances on the anniversary of her husband's death. The fact that she promised $10,000 to any one who provided the correct message generated much interest, but none of the medium's messages employed the secret code that Houdini had worked out before he died.

A message from beyond. Three years after Houdini's death, Arthur Ford, a medium who was the pastor of the First Spiritualist Church of New

Magician Harry
Houdini
demonstrates
how fraudulent
mediums manage
to fool the
unsuspecting
public.

York City, told his congregation that Houdini's mother was trying to make contact. "Forgive," Ford claimed, was the message Houdini's mother wanted to relay to Bess. When Ford contacted her, Bess confirmed that "forgive" was indeed the secret message Houdini had planned to communicate from the spirit world. But Ford committed a telling mistake: He, too, claimed that Houdini's mother had called her son "Harry."

Ford's representatives, it turns out, had already met with Bess Houdini. Suffering from both a high fever and a concussion, she was in a semi-delirious state when Ford's people visited her in the hospital; it's quite possible that Bess could have imparted the "secret" message while in this mentally hazy state. Adding to the possibility that Ford picked up on the "secret" word is the fact that the word had been published about a year earlier in an issue of the *Brooklyn Eagle*. Bess may also have conspired with Ford, as some suggest.

Houdini's believe it or not. A few days after conveying the "message," Ford staged a seance in Bess Houdini's home. While supposedly in a trance, he repeated the entire coded part of the message. "Rosabelle, answer, tell, pray, answer, look, tell, answer, answer, tell"—Houdini's code for the word "believe"—seemed to be the spirit of the magician urging his wife (whose nickname was Rosabelle) to believe Ford's message.

While Bess believed that only she and Houdini knew the code, a magician by the name of Joseph Dunninger said otherwise: The code had been published on page 105 of Harold Kellock's biography of the magician, *Houdini: His Life Story*. Much of Houdini's life, in fact, was an open book: "Rosabelle," Houdini's pet name for his wife, was engraved on the back of her wedding ring, which she had shown to many people.

Failure to communicate. While in the hospital, Bess Houdini told reporters that there were three messages from Houdini locked in her safe deposit box; these were copies of messages that Houdini was supposed to send from the spirit world. Bess was to receive one message, Remigius Weiss was to receive another, and Arthur Conan Doyle (the author of Sherlock Holmes stories) was to receive the third. Both men denied that Houdini had promised them a message from the spirit world. Although Bess had promised to reveal the messages, she never did, and her attorney claimed there were no messages in her safe deposit box.

Bess later claimed that she did not know what the exact message from Houdini was to be: She knew only that it was to be a ten-word message given in the magician's secret code. Although Ford eventually admitted to a reporter that he had obtained the code from Houdini's wife, Bess denied it and repeatedly stated that no one had yet produced her husband's message. The master magician, it seems, did not manage to escape from the spirit world. But he did manage to prove himself right: Anyone can talk to the dead, but the dead don't answer.

THE LEVITATION OF
DANIEL DUNGLAS HOME
- - - -

Daniel Dunglas Home, who lived from 1833 to 1886, was perhaps the most famous physical medium who ever lived. Because he never charged for his seances—although he did accept gifts and hospitality —few of his "victims" were eager to expose him.

Man Floats In and Out of Windows
Eighty Feet Above Ground!

Home frequently levitated. Witnesses said he seemed to float toward the ceiling in a semi-dark room. No one, however, actually saw Home levitate: Most people assumed he had risen because they felt his feet near their faces.

Home was occasionally involved in spiritualistic frauds. He was caught, for example, taking his foot out of his shoe during a seance. The dimly lit atmosphere of the seance allowed Home to create the illusion of floating above his seated guests. Having secretly placed his shoes on his hands, he waved his shoe-clad hands in the air to give his guests the impression that his feet were at eye-level. Participants also reported that his voice came from high up—an effect Home could accomplish simply by standing on a chair before opening his mouth to speak.

Home's most fearful feat. What was probably Home's most famous levitation took place in the presence of Lord Adare, Lord Lindsay, and Captain Charles Wynne in December 1868. Adare described what happened that day in his book *Experiences in Spiritualism with D. D. Home.* The spiritualist went into a trance, walked around the room, went into the next room, and opened the window. Lindsay, who thought he knew what was about to take place, cried out that what was happening was "too fearful ... He is going out of the window in the other room and coming in at this window." (Lindsay later claimed he knew this through telepathic communication.) At this point, Home appeared outside the window, opened it, and entered the room.

American Levitation: Home himself admitted that only one of his levitations occurred in daylight in Connecticut, at the home of Ward Cheney in August 1852. Yet, F. L. Burr, who reported this levitation, says that it occurred in "a darkened room." Why would Home mistakenly claim that the levitation had taken place in daylight? Perhaps he confused this levitation with another; or perhaps he wanted to keep non-believers in the dark.

He then asked Adare to close the window in the other room. When Adare found the window open only eighteen inches, he expressed his amazement that Home could have passed through such a narrow opening. Home responded by showing him how he had managed: He shot through the window head first and returned the same way.

The story of Home's levitation is usually reported in this manner, sometimes embroidered with additional details. The windows, for example, were said to be eighty dizzying feet above ground, and they were separated by a seven-foot span with only a four-inch-wide ledge between them. Adding to the difficulty of slipping in and out of the windows at eighty feet above ground level was the fact that each window was encased by a wrought iron balcony.

Floating Tables: Home also performed table levitations. Reports of his seances indicate that the table rose, uniformly, when people were seated around it joining hands on the table top. The table would then begin to rise, forcing whoever was seated to rise in order to maintain the circle of joined hands.

Home's levitating table might have been a trick, but it was no new trick. Fraudulent mediums had a history of using a device that consisted of a flat metal blade and straps that could be fastened to the arm under clothing. Two people on opposite sides of the table could engage the blades under the table top. Once the participants in the seance had placed their hands on the table, the two accomplices could announce that the table was rising. When they stood up, the table lifted with them--even though the circle of hands was unbroken--creating the illusion that the table was levitating.

The details don't add up. Parts of Home's story just don't make sense. The date and location of the levitation have been misstated. Although Adare reports that the light from outside the window was bright, there was a new moon—and therefore little light—on the night of the levitation.

And then there are the photographs of the building, which is no longer standing. They show two windows with balconies—only thirty-five feet above the ground—separated by what appears to be a mere four feet.

Two details make Home's levitation look even more suspicious. He consistently said that he had no control over his levitations, yet he told Adare and Lindsay that he was going out one window and in the other—a dangerous feat for someone aimlessly floating eighty feet above ground.

Apparently, Home had plenty of time alone in the building and could have practiced jumping from one balcony to the other. Or he might have created an illusion under the cover of darkness: After opening the window in one room he could have slipped out of the room to open the other window. Standing on the inside ledge of the second

Home stated that during levitation, he experienced a swollen and tingling sensation in his feet. He was usually lifted in an upright position, and his arms became rigid and drawn above his head as if he were grasping at some unseen power that was lifting him up from the floor. The spiritualist claimed to have remained levitated for as long as four to five minutes.

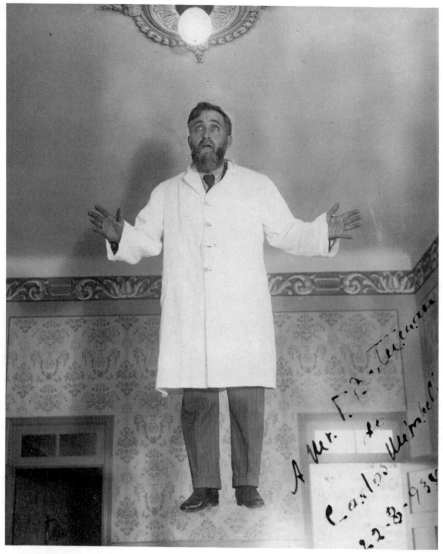

```
Mirabelli Floats! (... with the aid of a stepladder, airbrushed out
of the photo.)
```

window in the dark, he might have fooled a gullible witness into believing that he was actually standing outside the open window.

Mirabelli Floats. The only known photograph of a person actually levitating was the 1935 photo of the Brazilian medium Carlos Mirabelli (see page

58). Clad in a white lab coat, Mirabelli appeared to be rising to about six feet in the air with his arms lifted at his sides.

The Brazilian medium's secret? A stepladder. The original print, recently discovered, appears to show Mirabelli standing on the top step of a ladder that was clumsily airbrushed out. The alterations were concealed by the flowered pattern of the wallpaper in the room.

THE SOAL AND LEVY HOAXES

- - - -

Dr. S. G. Soal and Dr. Walter J. Levy were parapsychologists who were interested in investigating extrasensory perception. Both performed experiments that seemed to provide impressive documentation of the existence of ESP.

Scientists Document Proof of ESP!

As a recent graduate of medical school, Levy was drawn to parapsychology rather than medicine. He moved to Durham, North Carolina, to join the Institute for Parapsychology, where he conducted a number of studies involving paranormal happenings. The director of the institute, Dr. J. B. Rhine, was impressed by Levy's energy, and in 1973, he appointed Levy as the new director of the Institute of Parapsychology.

Rumors of false data. In 1973, rumors began to fly: Levy, his colleagues suspected, had misrepresented or falsified data. But there was no hard evidence, at least not until the summer of 1974, when Levy was seen "hanging around" the computer during an experiment. This was odd since the equipment was fully automated and did not require Levy's attention during the experiment.

Suspecting foul play, laboratory workers decided to lay a trap for the institute's new director. By installing a second set of wires, they obtained a second set of data. If the results of both sets of data were not comparable, they would have evidence that Levy had tampered with the experiment. There was

Psychic Mice and Chicken Embryos:

Levy authored twenty studies between 1969 and 1974. His research included investigating the clairvoyant abilities of mice to jump or run faster to avoid an electric shock that they knew was coming although they did not know when or where the shock would come. He was also interested in finding out whether chicken embryos could use their minds (psychokinetically) to increase the amount of time a heat lamp, which supplied them with warmth, was turned on.

little doubt that Levy had a hand in tampering with the data: A hidden observer saw him manipulate the equipment so that the computer would register a string of "hits." The second set of data, on the other hand, showed only random scoring.

Levy confesses to fraud. When Rhine got wind of the lab workers' findings, he immediately confronted Levy with the evidence. Levy confessed to fraud, but insisted that he had falsified only recent experiments. Blaming his lapse in ethics on being "overworked," he found little sympathy; Levy was fired shortly thereafter.

Soal's Experiment:

Soal's experiment consisted of five cards with a picture of an animal (such as a lion, elephant, giraffe, pelican, or zebra), placed face down in front of the subject. One number from one to five would be displayed, and the subject was asked to guess which animal was pictured on the card bearing that number.

Researchers began to question all of Levy's previous research, and it soon became clear that fraud was a common theme in his studies. James Terry, who had worked with Levy on some of his early research, was alarmed by these developments. Terry called Rhine to urge him to repeat all the work he had done with Levy, and Rhine agreed—at least for the time.

Terry's first attempts to reproduce Levy's findings showed no significant evidence of ESP. Rhine refused to allow Terry to publish his results, nor did he allow the researcher to publish a whole series of results that failed to reproduce the positive results of Levy's experiments. Eventually, Terry went over Rhine's head; Charles Honorton, the president of the Parapsychological Association, allowed Terry to report his results at an association annual meeting.

Soal Searches for Signs of Extrasensory Perception (ESP)

By conducting card-guessing experiments, Dr. S. G. Soal set out to reproduce the results of J. B. Rhine's earlier work in ESP. Starting in 1934, Soal tested 160 people. Conducting 57,000 telepathy trials and 70,000 clairvoyance trials, he failed to show any significant presence of ESP. He did, however, discover some startling results: Participants seemed to "guess" a card correctly when it came immediately *before* or *after* the correct card to be guessed.

Soal analyzed the tests of a man named Basil Shackleton, whose scores indicated that he "hit" the target card only by chance. However, when Soal analyzed Shackleton's results for one card before or one card after the intended target, he discovered scores significantly above chance.

Soal retests two subjects. In 1940, Soal sought out Shackleton for further experiments. He also retested Gloria Stewart, a subject who had shown the same significant tendency to score above chance. Soal reported his results in 1943, and repeated them, in summary form, in 1954. In all, Soal had conducted some 12,000 trials with Shackleton and 50,000 trials with Stewart in this new set of experiments.

Witness claims Soal fudged data. Several years later, Gretl Albert, who had been present at some of the trials, reported that she had seen Soal alter some of the responses in ink while the experiment was being run. Soal denied the accusation. An examination of some of the score sheets—some of which were supposedly lost—revealed no obvious alterations. However, the numbers Soal had supposedly used to randomize the trials were analyzed by computer; the results did not match any table of random numbers that was tested. What's more, computer examination of other aspects of Soal's results showed more irregularities.

Clearly, Soal's data was manipulated. We don't know how it was done, or whether Soal consciously altered the data, but we do know that Soal's card-guessing data offers no concrete proof of the existence of extrasensory perception.

Haunted Houses
Cryptic Curses
and Future
Forecasts

THE AMITYVILLE HORROR

- - - -

No one knows exactly what happened at the Dutch colonial house on Ocean Avenue in Amityville, New York, in 1975 and 1976. The best-selling—and supposedly nonfiction—book and movie about the haunting do little to resolve the Amityville mystery; as a matter of fact, they add to the confusion surrounding the supernatural story.

Haunted House Frightens Family of Five!

Few sources agree on the facts concerning the "Amityville Horror." What we do know is this: On November 13, 1974, Ronald DeFeo killed six members of his family in the house on Ocean Avenue. Tried and convicted, he failed to convince the judge that he had obeyed voices that had told him to kill, and he was sentenced to six consecutive life terms.

The price was right. In November 1975, a realtor showed George and Kathy Lutz the house on Ocean Avenue. Although they had been informed of the colonial's grisly history, the price was right, and they decided to purchase the Amityville home.

On December 18—the day the Lutzes moved in with their three children—they supposedly had a priest bless the house. During his blessing, the priest is said to have heard a loud voice say "Get out!" Less than one month later, the Lutzes moved out, leaving their possessions behind.

Money trouble. Even though George's business was not doing well, the Lutz family managed to finance the $80,000 Amityville home. In over his head with an unsound purchase, George soon realized that he could not continue to make his house payments. The Lutzes needed a way out of their financial troubles, and a haunted house looked like just the ticket.

Meanwhile, William Weber, the lawyer for murderer Ronald DeFeo, was trying to have his client cleared of murder charges by reason of insanity. When that didn't work, he planned to have DeFeo change his tune: "The devil made me do it" was to be the murderer's new line of defense.

Six bodies were found shot in the house on Ocean Avenue in Amityville, New York.

It isn't clear who first came up with the idea of a haunted house on Ocean Avenue; there is little doubt, however, that the plan gradually evolved among the Lutzes, lawyer Weber, and Paul Hoffman, the first writer to publish anything about the creepy colonial.

***Amityville*—the book.** Jay Anson, a writer who had worked on the screenplay of *The Exorcist,* was brought in to tell the Amityville story. Although he was not allowed to enter the house and never even interviewed the Lutzes, he did have a series of tapes in which the family outlined their account of the horror on Ocean Avenue.

Anson got a bit carried away. Borrowing heavily from *The Exorcist,* he allowed his imagination to author the book. And he was careless about details: In his rush to complete the book, Anson wrote a story full of contradictions. The floor plan of the house, for example, changed several times in later printings of the book.

Anson's book is also chock-full of outright falsehoods. Lutz admits that no one in his family ever saw the face of a pig. No marching band ever paraded through the house and no heavy door was torn off its hinges. No levitation occurred while Lutz was awake—although he admits that he might have dreamed it. The house was not built on a graveyard of the Shinnecock Indians. No windstorm or heavy snowstorm occurred on the nights that the book says they did. Nor was a policeman ever called to witness the cloven-foot tracks in the snow.

In a transcript of a trial that was held in September 1979 (*Lutz v. Hoffman*), the Lutzes admitted that almost everything in the book by Jay Anson was fiction. In fact, whenever the Lutzes, Anson, and Weber had to swear under oath about the so-called facts in the Anson book, no one could confirm any of the strange happenings as they are portrayed in *The Amityville Horror.*

The story of the Amityville horror couldn't be further from the truth. The fact is, the Lutzes—haunted by financial woes—became involved in a haunted house hoax for profit. And the supporting players in the scam did a superb job of selling the hoax to the public: Few people know that the whole episode was a hoax. Although the Amityville horror has been exposed as a fraud on a number of occasions, no exposure has ever rivaled the popularity of the book and movie that recount the fictitious haunting of the house on Ocean Avenue.

Family plagued by gawkers. Nothing out of the ordinary ever happened to the Cromartys, who moved into the house after the Lutzes abandoned it. The new owners did, however, sue the Lutzes because they were plagued by an onslaught of sightseers who stopped to check out the infamous address. The Lutzes settled out of court for an undisclosed amount.

The House of Blood: In the summer of 1987, a number of newspapers reported on a house in Atlanta that was oozing blood through the walls, ceilings, and floors. The blood was reportedly human. It seems the story was blown out of proportion. Several squirts of blood--such as might be found if a single intravenous bag of blood were squeezed a few times--were found in several rooms of the house. The blood did not match the type of either of the elderly occupants of the house. It *probably* came from another member of the family who was undergoing kidney dialysis; this person might have unwittingly squirted blood from the vessel to which the dialysis tubing was connected. Satisfied by this explanation, the police pronounced the House of Blood to be a case closed.

THE HOPE DIAMOND CURSE

John Baptiste Tavernier brought the Hope Diamond—originally a 112.5 carat blue diamond—from India to France in the sixteenth century. Although he would not reveal where he found the diamond, it was rumored to have been stolen from the eye of a religious idol in a temple in Mandalay, Burma. Somewhere along the way, the diamond earned a reputation for being cursed: Anyone who owned the magnificent jewel, so the curse said, was sure to meet an untimely end.

Spectacular Diamond
Dooms Its Owners to Death and Devastation!

Big Rocks: The value of a diamond is determined by demand, beauty, durability, rarity, freedom from defects, and perfection of cutting. The basic unit of weight is a carat, which is 200 milligrams; a well-cut round diamond of one carat measures almost exactly one-quarter of an inch in diameter. Even at its original size, the Hope Diamond would not be the world's largest stone. The Cullinan Diamond, discovered in 1905 in South Africa, weighed 3,106 carats before it was cut into nine major stones and ninety-six smaller gems. Cullinan I, also known as the "Greater Star of Africa" or the "First Star of Africa," is a pear-shaped diamond weighing 530.2 carats. Cullinan II, the "Second Star of Africa"--an oblong stone that weighs 317.4 carats--is set in the British Imperial State Crown.

When Tavernier first brought the stone to France, it was purchased by the only man in France who could afford it—the Sun King, Louis XIV (who reigned from 1643 to 1715). Tavernier, whose business had failed, eventually died in Russia. Louis lived to old age and passed the 112.5-carat rock on to his descendants. When Louis XVI (who reigned from 1774 to 1792) inherited the diamond, he presented it to his wife, Marie Antoinette. Both suffered a bit a bad luck when they lost their heads—to the guillotine—in the French Reign of Terror.

A mysterious disappearance. The diamond disappeared, probably stolen during the French Revolution, and eventually surfaced in London, England, having shrunk to 44.5 carats in size—still a sizeable rock. No one knows what happened to the remainder of the diamond, which might have been cut into smaller fragments.

Hope purchases diamond. After banker Henry Hope bought the diamond (which now bears his name), he lived to a normal age without any noticeable ill effects from its "curse." When

Hope died, the diamond was passed on to members of his family without causing any untimely deaths or spates of bad luck.

Only May Yohe, the wife of Lord Francis Hope, complained that the diamond brought her bad luck. The Hope family had sold the jewel in 1901, and in 1938, Yohe died in poverty due to bad investments.

Forty-four carat bad luck. After the Hope family sold the family jewel, hard times befell the rock's many owners. Of the next two owners—both of whom were jewelers—one went bankrupt and the other killed himself. The Russian nobleman who owned it next was stabbed to death by Russian revolutionaries. A Greek jeweler who owned it fell off a cliff, and the stone's Turkish owner—a sultan—was removed from his throne.

Eventually, Cartier's sold the jewel to Edward B. McLean, an American newspaper heir. More bad luck followed. McLean's only son was struck and killed by a car. His wife, Evalyn, divorced him, and he was committed to a men-

The Hope
Diamond.

tal hospital, where he died. Evalyn McLean continued to wear the diamond, even though ill fortune continued: In 1946, the McLeans' daughter committed suicide. The following year Evalyn McLean died at an advanced age.

New York jeweler Harry Winston bought the diamond and displayed it for several years before he donated it to the Smithsonian Institution in 1958. The diamond made the trip from New York to Washington, D.C., with little fanfare: Winston sent the gem—which was registered and insured for $1 million—through the regular mail, and the stone arrived safely.

A hoax, a curse, or just a lot of bad luck? Many of the diamond's owners—such as Louis XIV, Evalyn McLean, Henry Hope, and Harry Winston—did not die young. Others who owned the diamond briefly were unscathed by the experience. Although there is no arguing that a number of the diamond's owners did hit rock bottom, there's no solid connection between ownership of

A rare profile: New York jeweler Harry Winston who never permitted photographers to capture him head-on admires the 44.5-carat Hope Diamond.

the Hope Diamond and early death. If there is a curse on the gemstone, it's slumbering safely in the Smithsonian.

THE CURSE OF KING TUTANKHAMEN

- - - -

I n 1922 Howard Carter discovered the tomb of Tutankhamen; what he found was one of the most magnificent treasures ever unearthed. Carter later described the moment of his astonishing find:

> Slowly, desperately slowly, it seemed to us, the remains of the passage debris that encumbered the lower part of the door was removed, until at last we had

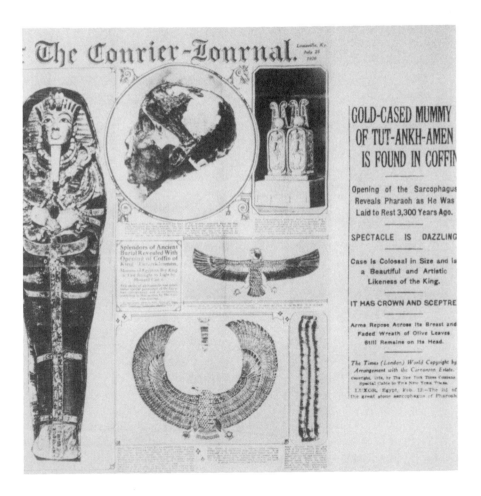

Newspapers around the world, like the Louisville, Kentucky, *Courier-Journal*, covered the opening of Tut's tomb.

the whole door before us. The decisive moment had arrived. With trembling hands, I made a tiny breach in the upper left-hand corner ... Candle tests were applied to precaution against foul gases and then, widening the hole a little, I inserted the candle and peered in. At first I could see nothing, the hot air escaping from the chamber, causing the candle flame to flicker but presently, as my eyes grew accustomed to the light, details of the room within emerged slowly from the mist; strange animals, statues and gold—everywhere the glint of gold. For the moment I was struck dumb with amazement, and when Lord Carnarvon, unable to stand the suspense any longer, inquired anxiously, "Can you see anything?" it was all I could do to get the words, "Yes, wonderful things!"

The Legendary Powers of the Pyramids:

The legendary powers of the pyramids have taken on the characteristics of a hoax. Originally, some people believed that the dimensions of the Great Pyramid (the Pyramid of Cheops) mirrored great mathematical relationships. From this came the idea that the structure of the pyramid itself formed some kind of coded message about the earth's future. This was all possible--according to some journalists--because the Great Pyramid was actually constructed by ancient alien astronauts.

Modern pyramid studies assert that placing a sharp object under a pyramid will preserve its sharpness, even with repeated use. They also claim that perishables such as fruit will not rot if they are placed under a pyramid, and that sleeping under a pyramid shape is somehow beneficial to one's health. None of these studies, however, produces reliable evidence to support the supposed miraculous effects of pyramid shapes.

Ancient Egyptian Boy King Curses All Who Enter His Sacred Tomb!

According to legend, anyone who entered the tomb of King Tutankhamen—best known as "King Tut"—soon died of an ancient curse that was inscribed as a warning at the entrance of the tomb. Today, nobody knows the whereabouts of the inscription, and it's possible that no one ever did. What's more, some of the people who first entered the tomb—including Howard Carter, the first to enter—lived many years after visiting the resting site of the ancient Egyptian king.

Scholars are not entirely sure who Tutankhamen was. He was probably the son of the infamous Akhenaten, who was king of Egypt for seventeen years (1379–1362 B.C.) during the Eighteenth Dynasty of the New Kingdom. His mother might have been Queen Kiya, one of Akhenaten's minor wives, who disappeared about the time that Tutankhamen was born in 1370. The nine-year-old king assumed the throne in 1361, after Akhenaten died, and married the dead king's surviving daughter,

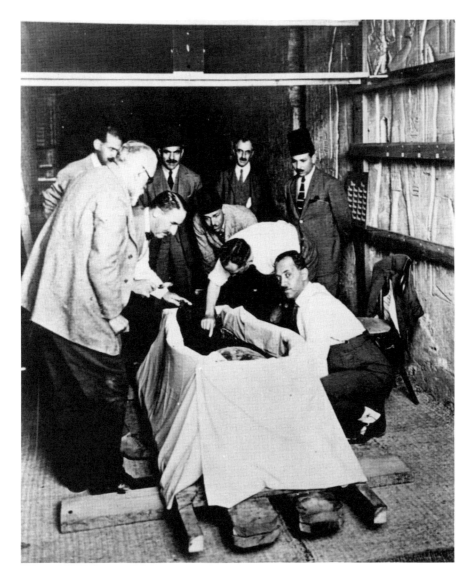

According to legend, the boy king cursed all who entered his sacred resting place, including the officials who examined his mummy.

Ankhesenpaaten. Tutankhamen ruled as king of Egypt until he died in 1352 at the age of eighteen. Today, the boy king known as King Tut is best remembered for the awe-inspiring treasure that was discovered inside his tomb.

A dead canary. It all began when Lord Carnarvon's pet canary died. The Lord, who sponsored an expedition to the tomb, died a little while later. At this

point, a French Egyptologist and occultist, J. S. Mardus, stated in a Paris news conference that the tomb contained "all the things which the priests and masters of the funeral ceremony were able to place in the way of protection against profaners [violators]." He also suggested that other curses had protected other tombs in the past, and mentioned deaths at other tombs as evidence.

Although a number of other people reportedly involved with Tutankhamen's tomb *did* die within a few years of its opening, many who were involved did *not* die shortly thereafter.

Herbert E. Winlock, the director of the Metropolitan Museum of Art in New York, tallied the number of people who had been present at the 1922 opening of the tomb who had died by 1934. The results were hardly staggering: Of the twenty-two people who were present at the opening, only six had died. Of the separate group of twenty-two people who had witnessed the opening of the King's sarcophagus in 1924, two died during the next decade. Ten people were present when the mummy was unwrapped in 1925, and all ten lived to tell about it in 1934.

The deaths of those who were present at the various openings were from natural causes. A few fell victim to diseases native to the area—not a startling fate for foreigners unaccustomed to local conditions.

The Pharaoh's curse. Reports that a curse was inscribed on the entrance of the tomb, or somewhere inside, were completely false: A carved or written curse was never found on or in the tomb. Yet somehow, the text of the curse fell into the hands of journalists eager to provide inquiring minds with the last word of the late King Tut.

NOSTRADAMUS'S PREDICTIONS

— — — —

Michael Nostradamus (Michel de Notredame) was a French physician of probable Jewish ancestry who lived from 1503 to 1566. His prophetic work, *The Centuries,* predicted what would happen in the future, and was probably first published in 1555.

Sixteenth-Century Physician Predicts Outcome of World War II!

Today there are no known copies of Nostradamus's 1555 edition of *The Centuries.* The work was arranged in quatrains—four-line verses, each consisting of two rhymed pairs—and the book was written in a form of medieval French that was antiquated even when Nostradamus wrote it. The text was vague, and could easily be translated and interpreted in different ways.

Not all verses present in modern editions of the book date back to Nostradamus's time. Some editions contain fifty-eight quatrains that were added sometime after the physician penned his predictions.

Nostradamus predicts the death of a king. What is probably the best-known quatrain supposedly predicted, in detail, the death of King Henry II of France, who lived from 1519 to 1559. It has been translated as follows:

> The young lion shall overcome the old
> On the field of battle in single combat;
> In a cage of gold he shall burst his eyes—
> Two fleets one, then to die, a cruel death.

Supposedly, Henry II was killed when he was pierced through the eye while jousting—and wearing a gold helmet—with a captain of his guard. But few of the details of his death match Nostradamus's predictions. The word "fleets" was later changed to "wounds," but Henry suffered only one wound. The forty-year-old king died when a splinter from the captain's lance penetrated his brain, not his eye. Still other sources say the splinter pierced his throat. The lion was the emblem of neither Henry nor his guard, and Henry's helmet was not gold. In short, the verses were hardly prophetic.

Yet another quatrain predicted great things for Henry II: The French king was to be "chief of the world" and would enjoy the title of "Victor." Nostradamus made these predictions in 1558, but Henry claimed no such fame before meeting his grisly fate the following year.

Small-town prophecies. Nostradamus was only interested in predicting things that would happen in his local area in the next few years. In fact, most of the references in *The Centuries* refer to events and places in France in the sixteenth century.

For example, one of the verses begins, "PAV, NAY, LORON." Some people have taken the words to be an anagram for "Napoleon"; in truth, however, they are the names of three neighboring towns (Pau, Nay, and Oloron) in southwestern France.

Documents dating directly to Nostradamus's lifetime prove that many of his predictions were just plain wrong. In a document written in 1564 by Catherine (mother to King Charles IX and Francis II) to Conetable (Catherine's godfather), she refers to predictions that Nostradamus had just personally divined for her. Conetable, the physician said, would live to be ninety, and so would Catherine's son, Charles; nevertheless, Conetable died at the age of seventy-seven and Charles died in 1574 at the tender age of twenty-four.

Nostradamus: A prophet with a poor success rate.

Nostradamus and the Nazis. In 1943 Karl Ernest Krafft, an astrologer for the Nazi party, wrote a small book called *Nostradamus prophezeit den Kriegsverlauf (Nostradamus Predicts the Course of the War)*. The book contains a great many "improvements" of the sixteenth-century verses and predicts that Germany would win World War II.

A number of verses supposedly predict Nazi leader Adolf Hitler's involvement in the war. Among them is verse II:24, which is correctly translated as follows:

Beasts mad with hunger will swim across rivers,
Most of the army will be against the Lower Danube.
The great one will be dragged in an iron cage
When the child brother will observe nothing.

By translating some of the medieval French words differently, some people discovered an entirely new meaning in the verse. They took the word "Hister"—an old name for a portion of the Danube River—to refer to Hitler, and they took "Germain"—a medieval French word for "brother"—as a reference to Germany. There is no way of telling what, exactly, Nostradamus meant, although educated guesses say that the verse refers to the Turkish advances in Hungary that occurred during the mid-sixteenth century.

A prophet with a poor success rate. Nostradamus's other verses have been carefully examined, and there is no reason to believe that any of them were meant to apply to events beyond the mid-sixteenth century. As for the physician's predictions for his own century, he was usually wrong. But generations of forgers and hoaxers have made a famous person of a false prophet.

THE TAMARA RAND HOAX
- - - -

Tamara Rand, a so-called psychic, claimed that she had predicted the March 30, 1981, assassination attempt on Ronald Reagan on a TV show in January of that year.

Psychic Predicts
Assassination Attempt on President Reagan!

The KNTV show *Dick Maurice and Company* had aired in Las Vegas, Nevada, on January 6, 1981—more than two months before John Hinkley's attempt on President Reagan's life. The psychic predicted that she saw the president shot in the chest at the end of March or early April by a young, fair-haired man who acted alone. The young man would be from a wealthy family and would have the initials "J. H."

NBC's *Today* show and ABC's *Good Morning America* broadcast the tape on April 2, 1981. After carefully examining Rand's appearance, however, an

Taped
Jan 6, 1981

Psychic Tamara
Rand on KNTV's
*Dick Maurice
and Company.*
The interview
was actually
taped March 31,
1981, the day
after the
president was
shot.

Associated Press reporter discovered that the tape had actually been made in the Las Vegas studios of KNTV on March 31, one day *after* the shooting. Although Rand had, indeed, appeared on Dick Maurice's show in early January, she did not predict the attempt on Reagan's life at that time.

Talk show host helps psychic. With the assistance of Maurice, Rand attempted to restage her January appearance. Wearing the same dress, she tried to pass off her March "prediction" as part of the January segment of the television show.

Not everyone was convinced. An investigator noticed one dead giveaway: Rand wore different rings on her fingers on the "prediction" segment than she wore on the rest of the show. The microphones, too, were in slightly different positions.

When Maurice was confronted with this evidence, he admitted to the hoax—claiming it had been cooked up to boost the psychic's career—and was suspended from his show. Later, Rand also confessed.

The ABC and NBC networks, however, were not eager to admit that they had been scammed: It took a bit of prodding to convince them to retract their stories about the psychic's uncanny prediction. NBC later devoted an entire segment to the hoax, granting Rand's wish to become a celebrity psychic.

Globe-Trotting
and
Gallivanting

CHRISTOPHER COLUMBUS HOAXES

- - - -

Christopher Columbus (1451–1506) was known for a number of things, but he wasn't known as a hoaxer. Yet a number of hoaxes have been committed in his name, long after he died. These include scams regarding the whereabouts of his remains and phoney writings penned by impostors.

Christopher Columbus's Bones Are Missing!

According to tradition, Columbus was buried in the cathedral of Santo Domingo, in the Dominican Republic. His remains were brought from Seville, Spain, in the 1540s, along with those of his son, Diego Columbus, at the request of Diego's widow, who lived in Santo Domingo.

The British attacked Santo Domingo in 1655, and the remains in the cathedral were concealed and forgotten. Some remains, however, were dug up in 1795 and taken to Havana, Cuba, where Columbus was to be memorialized. Although the identity of the remains was unknown, "tradition" identified the old bones as the remains of Columbus.

Father and son burial vaults. It seems that from the 1540s until 1795, there were two Columbus family vaults in the cathedral of Santo Domingo. One housed the body of Christopher Columbus, while the other contained the remains of his son, Diego. Apparently, Diego's remains, which had been buried on the other side of the church's presbytery, were exhumed and taken to Havana. In 1899, the remains were returned to Spain because Cuba had just been given to the United States when Spain lost the Spanish American War—Spain wanted Columbus's remains to stay in Spanish territory.

The hoax seems to have begun in 1795 when the Archbishop of Santo Domingo could not find the actual coffin of Christopher Columbus. He did, however, find Diego's coffin, which lacked a nameplate. Intentionally or unintentionally, the coffin was said to be that of Christopher Columbus.

Round and round the world he went, but where his bones are, nobody knows.

In 1917, the two vaults were destroyed during the remodeling of the cathedral. One of them (Diego's) was thought to be empty, while the other, whose location was forgotten, contained the real remains of Christopher Columbus. Although Diego Columbus's remains were returned to the cathedral of Santo Domingo before going to Seville, the remains of Christopher Columbus have been lost. That means that any cathedral—including Santo

Domingo—claiming to own the remains of Columbus is guilty of hoaxing the public.

Columbus's Only Writings

A more complex hoax involving Columbus has to do with a letter he wrote to his friend Luis de Sant Angel in 1493, describing his first voyage to the New World. In a letter that was supposed to be several pages long, Columbus told of the native peoples that he encountered. A printed version of this letter, which now resides in the archives of Simancas, Spain, is believed to have been published in 1493. At the same time, Columbus wrote another letter to his friend Gabriel Sanchez; the authenticity of this letter is not questioned. These two letters represent the only writings of Columbus.

References to the letter. The text of the de Sant Angel letter was first mentioned in 1825 in the *Colleccion de Viages* (published in Madrid), by Navarette, a nineteenth century Spanish travel writer. At first, it was believed to be the same as the Sanchez letter, several editions of which had been translated into Latin and published as early as 1493. Neither printed Spanish text lists a publisher, a place of printing, or a date of printing.

Although the contents of the two letters are similar, they were supposedly written separately and addressed to two different people. Some scholars believe that de Sant Angel had the text of his handwritten letter from Columbus printed in order to be able to reach a wider audience. Author Henry Harrisse, however, disagrees: After carefully examining the de Sant Angel letter, he concluded that it was a hoax, produced in the nineteenth century, probably based on the Sanchez letter.

A Forgery By Any Other Name: It takes a great deal of knowledge of fifteenth-century typography to produce a good forgery. The forger of the Columbus letter made a number of telling mistakes that gave away the fact that the 1493 imprint date was false. His job was made much easier, however, by the publication of a facsimile of the Sanchez letter, which was issued in 1866 in Milan. That facsimile was produced by lithography; the forged version, too, might have been produced by lithography, although it is impossible to determine without looking at the original.

The letter is sold and a lawsuit follows. In 1891, the copy that was used to produce a facsimile in 1889 (a London edition) was sold to an American for about $5,000—a very large sum at that time. The letter's new American owner eventually brought a lawsuit in a New York court on the grounds that he had been sold a forgery. A number of bibliographers were brought in to testify. Few, however, had any real expertise in fifteenth-century Spanish printing.

Globe-Trotting and Gallivanting

Someone pointed out that the spacing between the lines in the printed letter was irregular; how this could happen in set type—in which each letter is set evenly on a block of lead—was difficult to explain. Additionally, the document included letters and letter forms that were not used in the 1490s.

Today, there are at least three different versions of the fake letter from Columbus to de Sant Angel. And no two letters are alike: Each letter has a different set of errors. It seems that by correcting the errors in previous letters, each forger introduced new errors. Author Henry Harrisse believes that Enrico Giordani of Milan was the original forger.

ROBERT PEARY AND THE NORTH POLE

On April 6, 1909, Admiral Robert E. Peary (1856–1920) claimed that he was the first person ever to reach the geographic North Pole. In spite of his questionable documentation, his claim was accepted, and Admiral Peary was hailed as a hero.

Explorer Lies About Reaching North Pole First!

A man by the name of Frederick A. Cook (1865–1940), however, did not regard Peary as a hero. Five days before Peary announced his success, Frederick Cook, who had been a surgeon on Peary's 1891 expedition, made his own announcement: He claimed that on April 21, 1908—nearly a year before Admiral Peary was supposed to have reached the North Pole—he had reached the site that had eluded so many other explorers. Mass confusion followed; two believable explorers were both claiming to be the first person ever to step foot on the northernmost point on earth.

Peary's Previous Attempts to Reach the North Pole: Robert Peary had led several previous attempts to reach the North Pole. After his first attempt (in 1891) failed, he tried an overland route through northern Greenland in 1892-1893. He failed again. Peary led another attempt in 1893-1895, and, in 1905-1906, he tried to reach the North Pole by ship. He failed yet again, although his last voyage did come within 174 miles of the Pole.

Fallen heroes. Peary's supporters started a campaign to discredit Cook's claim, and the surgeon's life was deliberately ruined. Eventually, Cook was discredited and jailed for financial fraud.

The National Geographic Society was Peary's strongest supporter. The Society continued to defend him faithfully until 1988, when the evidence made it

impossible to believe the admiral's story. Wally Herbert was hired to investigate and bolster Peary's claim, but what he found was shocking. After examining the poorly documented records, Herbert concluded that Peary had not been the first man to reach the North Pole; in fact, Peary never reached the North Pole. Yet Herbert, who was still inclined to believe the best of Peary, attributed the explorer's failure to document his expedition to incompetence rather than malice.

Author Dennis Rawlins then claimed to have found the records Peary made on the day he reached the Pole—records that Peary had said did not exist. Rawlins showed, by Peary's own calculations, that on April 6, 1909, Peary was 121 statute miles (or 105 nautical miles) short of the Pole. That was as far north as the arctic explorer ever ventured.

A secret in a safe deposit box. Peary apparently knew that he hadn't reached the North Pole. He gave his wife a document, saying that it was

Robert Peary and man's best friend.

important and could destroy Frederick Cook's claim. Unable to understand the document, Mrs. Peary placed the record in a safe deposit box.

Peary's calculations remained under lock and key until 1935, when his daughter sent a copy of the paper to Melville Grosvenor, the director of the American Geographical Society. The document forever changed the way that people would remember Robert E. Peary: Fifteen years after the explorer died, Peary's daughter—who believed the paper supported her father's claim—had unwittingly exposed her father's fraud.

Harry Raymond, an astronomer, finally deciphered the document. It seems Peary's notations referred to sextant readings, which helped the explorer to navigate by measuring altitudes of celestial bodies. According to his own calculations, Admiral Peary was about 200 nautical miles from the North Pole at the time he claimed to have arrived there.

Much fur flew when Fred Cook fished for fame.

Even after the document was deciphered, it was sealed and its contents were not revealed. When Rawlins found the document again in 1973, he released the information that proved Peary never set foot on the North Pole. Apparently, Peary was so inept at using his instruments that he never knew exactly where he was. But he must have known that he hadn't reached the North Pole: The sun does not rise and set in the sky at the Pole.

VIKING HOAXES

- - - -

Many people believe that the Vikings or other early visitors arrived in North America well before Columbus ever stepped foot on American soil. Evidence, however, is hard to find, and much of it can be easily dismissed. But two artifacts—the Vinland Map and the Kensington Runestone—were not quickly shelved: The yellowing old map and the characters carved in stone were just enough to convince some people that Viking voyagers had visited the New World.

Viking Explorers Beat Columbus to New World!

The Vinland Map, named after a territory in the New World, was found bound into a volume with two other manuscripts; one dated from the fifteenth century, while the other dated from the thirteenth century. There was no question that the map had been in the bound volume for some time since worm holes in the manuscript pages matched those in the map.

The map is drawn on a single piece of vellum—a fine-grained skin prepared for writing—and measures about eleven by sixteen inches, folded down the center. Drawn in ink, the map depicts the three known parts of the medieval world—Africa, Asia, and Europe. It was based on the kind of circular or oval style that was popular until the second half of the fifteenth century, and the names on the map are in Latin.

Vikings Visit Canada: L'Anse au Meadow in Newfoundland, Canada, contains the apparent remains of the only genuine Viking settlement in North America. The area is currently being explored.

The most striking feature of the layout is the depiction of two large islands in the upper left corner of the map. One, called Gronelada, is clearly Greenland. The other one, further west and labeled "Vinlanda Insula," is what led some to believe they had found evidence that Vikings (or others) had traveled to the New World before Columbus. If this map had been drawn before Columbus was born, it must have relied on the "discoveries" of other explorers who came *before* Columbus.

A look under the microscope. A number of map experts have argued that the names, the wormholes, and the style of the map all suggest that it is an authentic Viking map. Nevertheless, Yale University, which acquired the map in 1957, decided to have the map tested. In 1972, McCrone Associates of Chicago—a firm that specializes in scientific testing of suspected art and other forgeries—examined the map.

To begin with, the contents of the map were suspect. McCrone Associates noted that although the map depicts Greenland and its coastline accurately, it is highly unlikely that a fifteenth-century mapmaker would have had such knowledge.

The Round Tower at Newport, Rhode Island:

Some people believe the Round Tower at Newport, a haphazard field-stone masonry structure, to be of Viking origin. In 1948 and 1949, William S. God-frey, Jr., an amateur archaeologist, exca-vated the entire area around the tower. He found a number of artifacts, but they weren't from the Viking era. Rather, he discovered all sorts of colonial artifacts-- including a gun flint, which could not have been made until well after the Viking era-- *beneath* the supposed Viking structure. That rules out any possibility that the tower was constructed before Columbus was born. In fact, the "Viking" tower was surely built during the American colonial period, probably in the 1650s.

The firm also conducted microscop-ical and chemical investigations of the map. The microscopical examination revealed that the ink line that formed the outline of the countries was bor-dered along its length by a yellowish discoloration.

At first, this was attributed to the tendency for old ink to become discol-ored along its edges because parts of it have leaked into the fibers of the paper. But further examination produced another explanation for the yellowish marks: The discoloration on the map had a "body" of its own, and pieces of the "yellow" could be flecked from the line with a fine needle. Apparently, the black ink line had been drawn over a slightly wider yellow line that had been laid down first. In fact, in one spot, the black line had been carelessly drawn so that it did not match the yellow line.

Man-made pigment. Still other tests—with higher magnification and polarized light—showed particles of what turned out to be anatase in the yel-low "ink." Anatase is a mineral, but the small and regular size of the anatase particles indicated that these were of a man-made variety; a titanium white pig-ment, Anatase was not available before 1917.

The ink in the two manuscripts that were bound with the Vinland Map was also tested. The levels of titanium (of a natural sort) in these inks were much lower. In fact, they matched the levels found in real aged-iron gallate inks that were used at the time the map was supposed to have been composed.

In short, the two manuscripts really are genuinely old. The Vinland Map, on the other hand, couldn't have been drawn before 1917. The forgers, it seems, made only one serious mistake: They used a yellow ink that was too modern for the 1400s.

The Kensington Runestone--
Runes Written in Stone!

The Kensington Runestone—a piece of flat sandstone about six inches thick, thirty inches long, and fifteen inches wide—was found in 1898 by farmer Olof Ohman, on his farm in Kensington, Minnesota. Entangled in the roots of a tree no more than thirty years old, the stone was covered on one side with what appeared to be sharply cut runes—the writing of the ancient Scandinavians. The writing, which has been translated by several experts in Norwegian language, is as follows:

Eight Goths and 22 Norwegians on an exploration journey from Vinland to the west. We had camp by 2 skerries one day's journey north from this stone. We were to fish one day after we came home found 10 men red of blood and dead AVM [Ave Maria]. We have 10 men by the sea to look after our ships 14 days' travel from this island Year 1362.

An ancient message in modern Swedish. Professor G. O. Curme, an expert in Germanic languages at Northwestern University, examined the stone. He remarked that it was odd that the stone, which dated itself to 1362, was written in modern Swedish with recent runes. He also noted that the cuts that formed the runes did not look old. With that, the stone was returned to Ohman.

Nine years later, a book salesman named Hjalmar Holand rediscovered the stone and spent the rest of his life advertising that it was an authentic

A Wealth of Viking Artifacts:

There are a great many supposed Viking artifacts from North America, including spears, axes, and swords. The axes are almost all socket-paring axes, a form of lumbering tool that has extra weight added to the butt for balance. Since this is strictly an American innovation, these axes can't possibly be of Viking origin. The small halberds (tobacco-cutting swords), which have been discovered in many places, were not used in Scandinavia until after 1500. These swords are in fact plug tobacco cutters, made in the nineteenth century in Ohio. Although several genuine Norse weapons of great antiquity were found in Canada, it was later shown that they were brought there from Norway in the early twentieth century.

FACE

ᛒ : ᛉᛟᛏᛁᚱ : ᛁᛉ : ᚠᚠ : ᚼᛁᚱ ᚱ ᛉᚼ : ᛒᛁ :
8   GÖTER   OK 22 NOR R   M EN   PÅ

ᛂᛒᛈᛉᛁᚱᛚᛈᚠᛉᚱᛒ : ᚠᚱᛂ :
OPDA GELSEF A RD FRÅ

ᛉᛁᚱᛉᛒ : ᛁᚠ : ᛉᛁᛏ : ᛉᛁ :
WINLAND OF   WEST WI

ᚼᛉᛂ : ᚱᛉᛉᛁᚱ : ᛉᛁᛒ : ᚠ : ᛈᛁᚠᛉᚱ : ᛁᛁ :
HADE LÄ GER WED 2   SKJA R EN

ᚦᛉᛈ : ᚱᛁᛈ : ᚼᛁᚱᚱ : ᚠᚱᛂ : ᚦᛁᛈ ᛈᛏᛈ :
DA G S RISE NORR FR Å THENO STEN

ᛉᛁ : ᛉᛉᚱ : ᛁᛁ : ᚠᛁᛈᛁᛁ : ᛁᛁ : ᚦᛉᛉᛉ : ᛉᛒᛏᛁᚱ :
WI WA R OK FI SKE EN DA G H ÄPTIR

ᛉᛁ : ᛁᛈᛉ : ᛉᛁᛉ : ᚠᛉᛉᛁ : ᛉᛉᛁ : ᚱᛟᛒᛈ :
WI KOM HEM F A N10 MA N RÖDE

ᛉᛈ : ᛒᚱᛈᛒ : ᛁᛉ : ᚦᛈᛒ : ᛉᚢᛗ :
A F BLOD OG DED A V M

ᚠᚱᛉᛁᛈ : ᛉᛈ : ᛁᛉᛈ :
FR Ä ELSE A F ILL Y

EDGE

ᚼᛉᚱ : ᛁ : ᛉᛉᚼᛈ : ᛉᛁ : ᚼᛉᛉᛁᛏ : ᛉᛏ : ᛈᛏ :
HAR 10 M A N S WE HAWET AT SE

ᛉᛒᛏᛁᚱ : ᛉᛁᚱᛁ : ᛈᛁᛒ : ᛁᚠ : ᚦᛉᛉ : ᚱᛁᛈ :
ÄPTIR WORE SKIP 14 DA G H RISE

ᚠᚱᛂᛉ : ᚦᛁᛈ : ᛟᛒ : ᛉ ᛂᚱ : ᛚᚠᛈᚠ :
FR ÅM THENO ÖH A HR 1362

NORMAL LATE RUNES.
ᚠᚢᚦᛂ ᚱᛉᛉᛏ ᛁᛉᛈᛏ ᛒᛉᛚᛉᛂᛁᛉᛒᛁᛉ
F. U. Th. O.   R. K. H. N. I. A.S.T.   B. M. L. Y. E. D. G. P. Æ. Ö.

THE KENSINGTON INSCRIPTION, WITH TRANSLITERATION AND STANDARD RUNES FOR COMPARISON

The Kensington Runestone.

Viking relic. His evidence, however, was less than reliable: He misquoted his sources, which were not readily available to those who listened to his defense of the stone. The experts were not impressed. After all, according to Norwegian language expert Professor Erik Wahlgren, the Swedish on the stone was a version of that language that had never been spoken anywhere outside the American Midwest.

A self-educated hoaxer. It looks like Ohman, a self-educated man, carved the stone himself. In fact, it even appears that his own speech peculiarities—reflected in his Halsingland dialect—were also present in the Runestone. He might have been helped by Sven Fogelblad, a former minister in Sweden, turned teacher, who knew runes well.

Ohman finally admitted that he knew how to read and write modern runes; he even had several books that illustrated runes. What's more, the Minnesota farmer was originally trained as a stone mason—a handy skill for a latter-day Viking.

Military
Maneuvers

H.M.S. *DREADNOUGHT*
- - - -

I n 1910, England was very proud of its navy. The Channel Fleet—also known as the Home Fleet—was assembled for review at Weymouth, a port on the English Channel. The admiral of the fleet, Sir William May, was on the flagship *Dreadnought*. Soon, Horace de Vere Cole, a prominent prankster, would join him on board as part of a royal party of hoaxers.

Phoney Ethiopian Royalty
Fool British Flagship and Fleet!

One February morning in 1910, de Vere Cole and his cohorts went—in full costume—to Paddington Station in London to catch a train to Weymouth. When the stationmaster was informed that members of the Ethiopian royalty were among the passengers at the London station, he arranged an impromptu reception for them on the platform.

While the group of hoaxers was on the train bound for Weymouth, another prankster (who has never been identified) sent a telegram to the admiral of the Channel fleet. Signed by the head of the British Foreign Office, the telegram informed Admiral Sir William May that a royal party was en route to Weymouth, and requested that he "kindly make all arrangements to receive them." This was news to the real head of the British Foreign Office, who did not learn of the forgery until days later.

When the "royal" party reached Weymouth, they were greeted with a red carpet welcome, complete with escort and car. After visiting a *Dreadnought* special launch in the harbor, they were taken to the flagship where the party met the admiral, inspected a marine guard, and toured the ship.

As a light rain began to fall, disaster seemed inevitable: The party's blackface makeup and fake mustaches would not withstand the February showers. Fortunately, when someone suggested to the captain that everyone would be more comfortable inside, he agreed.

The *Dreadnought* hoaxers.

Picky eaters and rented costumes. Once back on shore, the Ethiopians boarded another train. De Vere Cole—as Herbert Cholmondley of the Foreign Office—told the railroad personnel that the Ethiopian visitors would not eat unless they were served by people wearing white gloves. When the train stopped at Reading, several people rushed out to find a store that sold white gloves, and the Ethiopian party was later served by waiters in proper attire.

Once back in London, the Ethiopians paused for a group photograph, washed off their blackface makeup, and returned their rented costumes. Unable to keep the hoax secret, de Vere Cole went to the London newspapers with his outrageous story; the group photograph and the story of the hoax appeared in several newspapers. Although none of the names of the hoaxers were used, they were revealed in 1936 when Adrian Stephen's *The "Dreadnought Hoax"* was published.

Stephen's book prompted a number of groups, including Scotland Yard and the Admiralty, to consider launching an investigation. But since the pranksters were guilty of nothing more serious than sending a forged telegram, the investigations were dropped.

The Cast of Characters. Prankster Horace de Vere Cole enlisted the cooperation of a number of other hoaxers. Naturalist Anthony Buxton, artist Duncan Grant, brother and sister Adrian and Virginia Stephen (who was later known as the famous author Virginia Woolf), and Guy Ridley, the son of a judge, all answered the casting call for the *Dreadnought* hoax. Four of the pranksters, made up in blackface and dressed in Ethiopian robes, became members of the Ethiopian royalty. Buxton portrayed the emperor, while Cole, dressed in top hat and tails, played Herbert Cholmondley of the Foreign Office.

JOHN PAUL JONES AND THE AMERICAN NAVY
- - - -

John Paul Jones, a Scottish-born sailor who lived from 1717 to 1792, is usually given credit for founding the United States Navy. But credit—of some sort—belongs to Augustus C. Buell, the Jones biographer who made up the whole story.

John Paul Jones Wasn't Who People Thought He Was!

John Paul Jones, born simply John Paul, was drawn to the sea at an early age, becoming an apprentice seaman at the age of twelve. When he brought a merchant ship into port safely—after both the captain and the first mate had died—he was awarded 10 percent of the value of the cargo, and was given command of the ship.

After a difficult period as a captain, John Paul found himself in America, unemployed, at the beginning of the Revolutionary War. Having added "Jones" as his new last name, he obtained a position as an officer aboard the *Alfred*—the first naval ship bought by Congress—thanks to his acquaintance with a congressman. Jones was later given command of the *Providence,* where he earned a distinguished record.

A hero in the making. Promoted to captain and in command of the *Ranger,* Jones was sent to France. Sailing back and forth between France and the United States, he garnered quite a reputation. On his return trip to the United States, he managed to capture the British sloop *Drake,* taking many prisoners. Returning to France with seven "kills" and many prisoners to his credit, Jones was greeted as a hero. Later, in a journey around the British

John Paul Jones.

Isles, he captured seventeen ships, and then defeated the *Serapis* in an impressive bout.

Although political rivals blocked his promotion to admiral, Jones was awarded command of the *America,* the largest ship in the navy (which was then under construction). Although Jones never took command of the *America,* which was eventually turned over to the French, he received a gold medal from Congress and accepted an offer from Catherine the Great to serve in the Russian navy.

A proper burial and the sailor's biographer. Quite ill, Jones spent the last two years of his life in Paris. Buried in a French cemetery that was eventually taken over by housing, his body was shipped back to the United States in 1905. Eight years later, his remains were buried in a specially constructed tomb at the U.S. Naval Academy in Annapolis, Maryland.

In 1900, Augustus C. Buell published a two-volume history titled *Paul Jones, Founder of the American Navy.* The writer's background, however, left something to be desired: His statements about his own history were often, in a word, inaccurate. In fact, Buell, who has been labeled a "fraudulent historian," manufactured the misinformation about Jones's role in the founding of the United States Navy.

Libraries in the sky. Scholars' reactions to Buell's biographies were mixed. Some praised his new "discoveries" while others concluded that he had located material that was no longer available. Librarians and archivists, however, had no luck finding the documents Buell claimed to have discovered in their libraries. The biographer, it seems, had provided himself with a clever "out": Because Buell claimed that one of his ancestors had known the subject of his biography, some scholars concluded that he must have consulted a family archive to research his books. The trouble was, no such archives existed.

In 1906, in the first exposé of Buell's biography of John Paul Jones, author Anna De Koven stated that the book

is based upon a bare framework of truth ... but is padded with inventions of clever construction and unparalleled audacity. It contains reports of imaginary committees in Congress, invented letters from Washington, Franklin and Hewes, false letters and imaginary journals of Jones himself, false entries in the diaries of well-known persons such as Gouverneur Morris and the Duchesse d'Orleans, and quotations from others which existed only in Colonel Buell's imagination.... The bibliography ... is a masterpiece of inven-

Biography as Fiction: Augustus C. Buell also wrote the biographies of Sir William Johnson, William Penn, and Andrew Jackson. He claimed to have ancestors who had worked for, or who had known, all of the men he wrote about. All of Buell's biographies contain statements that are taken from documents that were made-to-order by the author himself: He freely invented letters, journal entries, books (usually described as quite rare), and even whole archives. Although Buell thanked the Library of Congress for making materials available to him, some scholars question whether the phoney biographer ever set foot inside the hallowed halls of that repository.

tion, and is so shortsighted in its careless untruthfulness as to raise suspicion of the author's mental responsibility.

A clever dog. Samuel Eliot Morison, the author of the latest biography of Jones, devotes several pages to a list of Buell's false statements about Jones. About the writer, he says:

> He found it easier to write Jones' letters himself than to use the genuine ones in the Library of Congress, which he never visited. How, then, did Buell acquire such a high reputation? He was a clever dog, wrote good salty prose and supported his statements by references to mythical sources and fictitious books, which gave his work an air of scholarly authenticity. Any librarian ... will do a service to posterity by reclassifying as fiction Buell's book [on Jones].

THE MAN WHO NEVER WAS
- - - -

The Man Who Never Was is one of the most complex and clever military scams ever to fool enemy intelligence. The hoax, known as Operation Mincemeat, was masterminded by Ewen Montague during World War II.

Operation Mincemeat
Fools German Military Intelligence!

Montague devised the hoax because the Allied forces wanted to divert the attention of Nazi leader Adolf Hitler and Italian dictator Benito Mussolini away from the upcoming allied invasion of Sicily, Italy. By making the Germans believe that the invasion would take place from Greece and Sardinia, the Allied forces would improve their odds for launching a successful attack.

The plan called for the body of someone who had recently died of drowning or pneumonia and whose corpse could be used by British Military Intelligence. They would then dress the body in a British Marine officer's uniform, put the I.D. of Major William Martin on its body, and chain a briefcase containing "top secret information" to the body's wrist. The corpse was to wash ashore at Huelva, Spain, where active German agents mingled among the Spanish. The body would appear to have come from a ditched airplane and would be accompanied by a life raft.

A long search produced just such a body whose owner had died of pneumonia. After securing permission to use the body, military personnel stored the corpse in refrigeration until the Man Who Never Was was ready to make his public debut.

The Man Who Was--Ewen Montague.

Since dropping the corpse from an airplane could damage it, Operation Mincemeat called for a submarine to release the body into the water. A torpedo-shaped canister was built so that it would release the body when opened. The canister also contained dry ice in order to drive out the oxygen that would speed up the body's decomposition.

Major Martin lands in Spain. After much difficulty, including getting the boots on the corpse's feet, among other things, the container with the body and briefcase was loaded aboard the submarine *Seraph*. The sub proceeded to the planned site, where the body was removed from the canister and "launched" toward shore. Days later, the naval attaché in Madrid sent a signal that Major Martin's body had been recovered off Huelva.

The British issued urgent requests through Spanish diplomatic channels to ensure the return of all the papers that Martin was carrying. All of the supposed courier's papers were returned—eventually. Tests showed, however, that the letters had been opened and resealed. Major Martin was buried in Spain, and his name and those of his plane's crew were added to the list of casualties for the week.

Personal Effects of the Man Who Never Was:

Major Martin carried a briefcase that contained letters of transfer from various generals. The letters made it clear that Martin was being sent to North Africa because of his expertise on amphibious barges. The briefcase also contained several letters from his father and from his fiancee, Pam, as well as an unpaid bill for an engagement ring and a notice that the bill for his lodging was overdue all designed to make Major William Martin look like a regular guy. He also carried the proofs of a military publication, with a letter to General Dwight Eisenhower, requesting that he write introductory material for the American edition. Last, but far from least, he carried secret letters that revealed that the real allied attack would come not from Sicily, but from Sardinia and Greece.

Mincemeat is swallowed whole. As the hoaxers had expected, the information in the secret letters was sent to Berlin, where the German intelligence service fell for it, hook, line, and sinker. A cablegram informed Winston Churchill (then British prime minister), "Mincemeat swallowed whole." When the Allies invaded Sicily, they encountered little in the way of resistance. Most of the defenses that the enemy had stationed in Sicily were relocated to the northern end of the island.

After the war, an examination of captured German naval intelligence files turned up a German translation of the secret letters that named Greece and Sardinia as the sites of the allied invasion. Admiral Doenitz, the commander in chief of the German navy, had initialled the letters to indicate that he had read them.

About that time, Doenitz met with Hitler, who did not think that the Allied forces would attack Sicily first. Furthermore, General Rommel was sent from Italy to Greece to take charge of operations there—as if the Nazis were expecting an allied attack on Greece. Operation Mincemeat was a success, and the Man Who Never Was will forever be remembered in military history.

Weird Science
and
Bad Medicine

DARSEE, SUMMERLIN, AND RESEARCH FRAUD

- - - -

John Roland Darsee, a brilliant young physician, was working at one of the hospitals affiliated with Harvard Medical School in Boston in 1981. Known for the tremendous number of research papers he produced, Darsee studied the heart muscle of heart-attack patients. His research indicated that much of the injured heart muscle could be restored to function after a heart attack.

William T. Summerlin worked at the Sloan-Kettering Institute for Cancer Research in New York City in 1974. At a meeting of science writers, Summerlin told journalists that "after human skin is maintained in organ culture for four to six weeks, it becomes universally transplantable without rejection." It looked like the major obstacle to transplantation had been overcome. As it turns out, Summerlin and Darsee each did considerable damage to biomedical research by submitting fraudulent accounts of their research experiments.

Scientists Fake Results of Ground-Breaking Research!

Although John Darsee obviously worked quite hard, many people, especially his coworkers, wondered how he could produce such a large volume of research—research that would normally be very complicated and time-consuming. One evening in May 1981, they secretly watched as Darsee forged raw data for an experiment that he was about to submit for publication. It seems that when his supervisor asked for the raw data, Darsee went into a laboratory and proceeded to make up the data. Although he confessed when he was confronted about the phoney results, Darsee claimed that this was the only experiment he had ever faked.

Stripped of his Harvard appointment, Darsee was allowed to continue working in the laboratory, and he continued to contribute abstracts and

papers. Darsee's coworkers, however, were still suspicious. National Institute of Health (NIH) inspectors, too, began to suspect the prolific scientist: Part of his funding had come from the NIH, and investigators began to suspect that Darsee had a history of fraud.

A blue ribbon panel was formed at Harvard in early December 1981, in order to look into the matter. What they found did not look good: Darsee could not produce any raw data for studies he had conducted after his first year at the laboratory—that is, after his lab work was less carefully supervised.

The "Golden Hands" Hoaxer:

Mark Spector made up college degrees that he didn't have, and he almost earned a doctorate from Cornell University in 1981. Because only he could get some experiments to work, he was known for his "golden hands" in the laboratory. This should have aroused suspicion, but it didn't at first. Spector's work provided, among other things, a basis for a unified theory about the cause of cancer. But when Spector's notebooks were inspected for raw data, they were full of data that had been written in, without printouts from the electronic equipment that was analyzing the samples. His fraud discovered, Spector was dismissed from Cornell without a doctoral degree. Investigators later discovered that both Spector's B.A. and M.S. degrees were fakes.

The blue ribbon panel's report. The panel's report cleared Harvard of any blame for having allowed Darsee to continue his research in the lab for six months after his initial fraud was discovered. As it turned out, two studies conducted during that six-month period contained data that were "highly suspect," and Darsee was forced to resign from the Sloan-Kettering laboratory.

Still more fraud lurked in the halls of science. After he received his M.D. from Indiana University, and before he arrived at Harvard, Darsee spent a number of years at Emory University in Atlanta, Georgia. After Darsee's forced resignation, Emory opened an investigation of his work. This was no small task: During his five years at Emory, Darsee had written ten papers and forty-five abstracts.

Most of Darsee's publications were suspect and had to be retracted; only two papers and two abstracts were allowed to stand. What's more, Darsee had apparently put the names of Emory scientists on his abstracts as coauthors, without their knowledge. It seems none of the "coauthors" had objected—that is, if they ever found out.

Suspicious breakthroughs in transplantation. Much of William Summerlin's work involved the transplantation of rabbit corneas. But his colleagues were suspicious: The eyes of the rabbits who were supposed to have received transplants were a bit too perfect.

Summerlin also produced two white mice with black patches on their skin. He told his supervisor, Dr. Robert Good, that the dark patches were areas of skin that had been transplanted from black-skinned mice. It seems that isn't exactly how Summerlin had created the black patches: He had, in fact, inked the black patches on the mice with a felt-tip pen. When a lab assistant noticed the fakery and reported it to his superiors, Summerlin was immediately suspended from the laboratory.

Medical leave for exhaustion. Dr. Lewis Thomas, the president of Sloan-Kettering, set up a formal investigation. Having reviewed Summerlin's work, the investigating committee decided to terminate Summerlin's relationship with Sloan-Kettering. Good, on the other hand, was cleared of any role in the fraud.

In the end, Summerlin, who claimed that he had been forced into fraud because of the intense pressure on him to produce, was given a period of medical leave, with pay, so that he could recover from what was called "exhaustion."

RORVIK AND THE CLONING OF A MAN
- - - -

S cience journalist David Rorvik enjoyed a respectable reputation. When he published *In His Image: The Cloning of a Man* in 1978, the public was fascinated. Many people accepted Rorvik's claim that a human being had been cloned, but the scientific community was not convinced.

Journalist Discovers
Boy Cloned in Tropical Laboratory!

Scientists were reluctant to believe Rorvik. They knew that technology was not sufficiently advanced to produce a human clone, and Rorvik produced no documentation to persuade them otherwise. To make matters worse, Rorvik did not supply adequate documentation to convince the scientists that human cloning had occurred.

In his book, Rorvik claimed to have received a phone call from an elderly millionaire called "Max." Rorvik had previously been the science editor for *Time* magazine, and Max was familiar with Rorvik's writings about human reproduction and cloning.

The millionaire, it seems, was interested in cloning himself, and was willing to shell out a tidy sum to do it. With millions of dollars as his incentive, Rorvik found a willing scientist, "Darwin," who was a gynecologist.

Darwin and Rorvik set up a lab in a tropical country where native women—who supplied the eggs to be fertilized—would attempt to carry the

embryo clone to term. The nucleus of a cell from Max's body was transferred to a cell without a nucleus from "Sparrow," the selected "mother." When Sparrow carried the embryo to term and delivered a boy in the United States, millionaire Max had a perfect clone of himself.

A lawsuit against Rorvik's publisher. In his book, Rorvik mentioned Derek Bromhall, a British scientist, as the man who had developed the scientific basis for cloning; the public took this as proof for the claim that a human cloning had occurred. In 1978, however, Bromhall sued J. B. Lippincott, the publisher of Rorvik's cloning book, claiming—in federal court—that his reputation had been harmed by the book. Bromhall accused Rorvik of quoting from his doctoral dissertation, which explored the possibility of human cloning; Rorvik was not authorized to quote the scientist's research.

Bromhall pointed out a number of problems with Rorvik's book. For instance, the cloning process that Rorvik described (very vaguely) was theoretically impossible as it was outlined in the book. It seems that Rorvik did not understand cloning research, and many of the errors in his book stemmed from this lack of understanding.

Of frogs and men. In the mid-1960s, scientists had successfully cloned a frog. Cloning a human being, however—as Bromhall noted—posed a different set of problems. A frog's egg is much larger than a human egg and is therefore easier to work with.

Rorvik claimed that the nucleus of the donor egg was removed by treating it with the chemical Cytochalasin B. The trouble is, although this chemical will remove the nucleus of some cells, it will not enucleate an egg cell.

More reason to question Rorvik's book. Rorvik's book was printed by the publishing company's trade division, not by the medical division. While the trade division simply accepted Rorvik's reputation, the medical division could have had outside experts review the manuscript. What's more, Rorvik's timing was off. Several months after the cloning was supposed to have been done, the journalist was still trying to get information from Bromhall about his cloning methods.

A fraud and a hoax. Based on this evidence and on the testimony of court experts, Judge John Fullam ruled that the book was "a fraud and a hoax." He said that the plaintiff had finally and conclusively established that "the cloning described in the book never took place" and that "all of the characters mentioned in the book, other than the defendant Rorvik, have and had no real existence." In 1982, Bromhall settled his case against Rorvik out of court, for an undisclosed sum. Part of the settlement agreement required Rorvik (who continued to deny that the book was a hoax) to apologize to Bromhall.

Biochemical Breakthrough or Bust?

Rorvik claimed that, to speed up the success rate of cloning a human, the experiment included a number of "serial transfers" of one nucleus to another. Scientists know that this can't be done because only a colony of cells would exist. Yet Rorvik claimed that "biochemical breakthroughs" allowed the serial transfers to succeed. If these breakthroughs had really taken place, modern medicine would be able to tackle a number of thorny problems, such as cancer, tissue regeneration, and transplantation. Could a scientist and a science journalist working in isolation in a small tropical lab have the equipment, technique, and knowledge to accomplish in one short period what thousands of scientists over the decades have tried unsuccessfully to do? The Nobel Prize committee doesn't seem to think so.

BIORHYTHMS

- - - -

In 1887, German physician Wilhelm Fliess probably invented the notion of biorhythms. Sometime around 1960, George S. Thommen, a Swiss importer, introduced the United States to biorhythms—not to be confused with biological rhythms, which are valid biological cycles.

Biorhythms Predict Every Waking Moment!

Fliess claimed that every body cell has a cycle that plays an important role in the peaks and valleys in an individual's vitality and mental and physical strengths. He believed that these cycles, or biorhythms, even determined the date when a person would die.

Fliess also claimed that everyone is basically bisexual. Characteristics he labeled as "male"—such as strength, courage, and endurance—functioned in a twenty-three-day cycle. "Female" characteristics—such as sensitivity, intuition, and love—were keyed to a twenty-eight-day cycle (which was different from the menstrual cycle).

In the 1920s, an Austrian engineer by the name of Alfred Teltscher added a third cycle to Fliess's theory; biorhythms were expanded to include physical, intellectual, and emotional cycles. Since a person's birthdate determined when these cycles started, biorhythms were connected to astrology; sometime around 1900, Herman Swoboda added an astrological aspect to biorhythms.

An s-shaped curve. According to biorhythm theory, the physical cycle lasts twenty-three days, the emotional cycle lasts twenty-eight days, and the intellectual cycle lasts thirty-three days. All of these cycles start at "zero" at the moment of birth, and follow an "s-shaped" curve thereafter.

The emotional cycle reaches its peak in seven days, and crosses the zero line in another week. It then declines for a week to its minimum

value, and rises again in another week. The cycle thus completes its curve within twenty-eight days.

Peak behavior and critical points. Biorhythm theory claims that when a cycle is above the zero line (positive), the abilities governed by it increase, and vice versa. This means that a person can have one, two, or all three curves positive, negative, or mixed on any given day. A person is at the peak of his or her behavior when all three curves are at their positive maximum.

On the other hand, when all three curves are at their lowest point, it's a good idea to stay out of harm's way. When a cycle line is crossing the zero axis, it is said to be at its "critical" point; this is when people are most apt to be involved in a catastrophe in that particular area of life. Human disasters, according to the theory, are most likely to occur to a person who experiences more than one critical cycle on a given day.

An unscientific approach and disappearing research. Neither Thommen, who introduced biorhythms to the United States, nor Gittelson, who wrote *Bio-Rhythm,* is a scientist. Neither understands what valid scientific research involves. Instead, they have relied on the stories of people who have had tragedies in their lives that occurred on days when more than one of their cycles were critical or minimal. Gittelson has commented that "the most convincing studies of biorhythm are those you can do for yourself."

Fliess, Swoboda, and Teltscher all claimed to have conducted studies to validate biorhythm theory; however, none of these studies exists. Swoboda claimed that his eight trunks of research notes were lost when the Nazis invaded Vienna. Teltscher's research was never published. And Fliess's contributions consist of stories taken from psychiatric interviews with patients contained in rare books that were never translated from German into English.

Sports stats and performance curves. Nevertheless, several people attempted to test biorhythm theory by using published sports statistics. Using an athlete's birthdate, researchers iden-

The Nose Knows:

Fliess's other "major" contribution to science was a theory that all illnesses were controlled by centers in the nose. The German physician believed that almost any condition could be treated by operating on the patient's nose.

What Goes Around Comes Around:

Biological rhythms are distinct from biorhythms. Many things in the living world display regular, cyclic behavior; most of these cycles are tied to the twenty-four-hour rotation period of the earth. The twenty-four-hour light and dark cycle or tidal cycle seem to be the "synchronizers" for these "circadian" rhythms, which are about twenty-four hours long and include activity cycles, feeding cycles, and sleeping cycles.

tified the athlete's biorhythm curves in order to compare them with his or her performance.

Studies that involved Arnold Palmer's golf tournament victories were quoted as support for the biorhythm theory. Supposedly, Palmer's physical curve would peak on the day of a "win," as long as the other two curves were not at the critical point.

After reexamining the data, skeptics discovered that incorrect statistical tests were applied to Palmer's victories. In truth, few of Palmer's wins were on days when his physical curve was high. And other studies of golfers' biorhythms failed to support the theory. In fact, the biorhythms of golfers on the dates they won tournaments showed results that did not differ from chance results. What's more, a study of the pitchers of no-hit baseball games arrived at similar results.

Studies of Arnold Palmer's tournament victories were quoted to support biorhythm theory.

Weird Science and Bad Medicine

Nevertheless, biorhythm calculators and books continue to flourish. In spite of the unsound theory behind biorhythms and unsuccessful scientific attempts to prove the theory, some people continue to believe in—and others continue to profit from—the theory of biorhythms.

MUNCHAUSEN'S SYNDROME
- - - -

Some people thrive on being admitted to the hospital—and even go so far as to have unnecessary surgery. These people are said to have "Munchausen's Syndrome," a disorder characterized by a chronic desire for unnecessary hospitalization or surgery.

Munchausen's Patients Crave Surgery and Hospital Care!

Munchausen's syndrome is named after the semi-fictional Baron Munchausen; although there really was a Baron named Munchausen, the book of his supposed adventures is a work of fiction. The fictional Munchausen was famous for lying dramatically about his adventures; similarly, those who suffer from the syndrome named for him are famous for lying—in a dramatic way—about their medical condition.

People who have Munchausen's Syndrome tend to be socially isolated, with no close family ties or friends. They often arrive at the hospital emergency room with what appear to be genuine emergency symptoms, and many have scars that indicate previous surgeries. Munchausen's patients usually leave the hospital early—against medical advice—and without paying their bills.

A familiar pattern. Munchausen's Syndrome is rather rare: Through 1990, there were about 200 known cases of the condition. Many patients are repeatedly admitted to the hospital—some as often as 100 times.

Author Loren Pankratz noted that these admissions often followed a pattern. Patients usually use the same symptoms from one hospitalization to the next, adding a minor symptom each time. Since they are usually familiar with medical terminology and hospital procedures, they are able to present a convincing case. Many Munchausen's patients are also drug abusers who deceive physicians in order to obtain prescription drugs.

What's In a Name? Munchausen's Syndrome was named by R. Asher in a 1951 *Lancet* article. Although the condition has recently been renamed "Chronic Factitious Illness," the old name remains popular.

Medical problems real and imagined. Many Munchausen patients

BARON MUNCHAUSEN's
N A R R A T I V E

OF HIS

MARVELLOUS TRAVELS

A N D

C A M P A I G N S

I N

R U S S I A.

HUMBLY DEDICATED AND RECOMMENDED

T O

COUNTRY GENTLEMEN;

AND, IF THEY PLEASE,

TO BE REPEATED AS THEIR OWN, AFTER A HUNT
AT HORSE RACES, IN WATERING-PLACES, AND
OTHER SUCH POLITE ASSEMBLIES ; ROUND THE
BOTTLE AND FIRE-SIDE.

O X F O R D:

Printed for the EDITOR, and fold by the Bookfellers there and
at Cambridge, alfo in London by the Bookfellers of Picca-
dilly, the Royal Exchange, and M. SMITH, at No. 46, in
Fleet-ftreet.—And in Dublin by P. BYRNE, No. 108, Craf-
ton-ftreet.

MDCCLXXXVI.

FIRST ISSUE OF BARON MUNCHAUSEN'S TRAVELS (*enlarged*)

First edition title page of Baron Munchausen's travel book.

do have some underlying medical problems. Others have faked their conditions by mixing blood into their urine specimens, by producing fevers through
injections, and even by injuring themselves, incurring serious cuts and bro-
ken bones.

Recently there have been reports of "Munchausen's Syndrome by
Proxy"—in which a parent hurts his or her children in order to get attention,

often from medical personnel. The children involved are often infants or toddlers who are too young to tell of their own symptoms or lack of symptoms.

What motivates a patient to behave this way is unclear. Surgical addiction, lack of money, and a tendency toward self-mutilation may all play a role in Munchausen's Syndrome. Munchausen's patients may also enjoy receiving pity in place of love—although guilt often prevents them from accepting the pity.

PSYCHIC SURGERY
- - - -

Psychic surgeons supposedly perform "surgery" that heals instantly and leaves no scar. After rubbing the part of the body that is said to be diseased, the "surgeon" reaches through the patient's skin with bare hands to remove tissue that is believed to be tumorous. The patient, seemingly cured, is then sent home considerably poorer.

Psychic Surgeons Work Miracles Without Scalpels and Knives!

Blood *seems* to flow as the psychic surgeon appears to remove tissue without the use of a scalpel. Trained magicians, however, have seen through the so-called surgeons' bogus operations. By observing the actual "operation" and films of the operation, magicians have discovered that the entire procedure is actually sleight of hand.

Magician James Randi perfected his own performance of psychic surgery to such an extent that he can't be distinguished from the psychic surgeons themselves. Randi—unlike the other psychic surgeons—admits that it is all a trick and he has revealed how it is done.

Popular Psychic Surgeons: Psychic surgery is most popular in Brazil and the Philippines, where it is a multi-million dollar a year industry. The best known psychic surgeons of the Philippines--"Arigo," whose real name was Jos Pedro de Freitas, and Antonio Agpaoa--treated several hundred people between them.

False fingers and cow's blood. The secret of psychic surgery lies in careful advance preparation. A false "thumb tip"—a standard item at magic supply houses—is essential. This rubber false finger, bigger and longer than a person's own thumb, fits over the real thumb. Inside the hollow thumb tip, a number of "props" can be stored, such as animal tissue; chicken, pig, or cow blood; chicken fat; and sinew. With the tissue and blood inside the hollow thumb, the surgeon can slip on the thumb tip when he or she picks up gauze bandages for cleansing. The surgeon can then squeeze the thumb tip for a flow of blood. Removing the tip to the inside of one hand, the surgeon can squeeze tissue out of the open end of the thumb tip.

When working on a heavy person's abdomen, the psychic surgeon can actually appear to place his or her hands inside the patient's body with the aid of some clever finger bending. At the end of the operation, the surgeon disposes of the thumb tip with the soiled and bloody gauze from the "operation."

A costly operation. Practice makes the psychic surgeon's movements very difficult to detect—at least for those who are not trained in magic and sleight of hand. However unlikely it may seem, people are fooled. Some have refused to see a regular physician to treat a real tumor until it is so advanced that it is no longer operable. In fact, a follow-up investigation of some of the people who were treated by psychic surgeons revealed that almost all of the patients died within a year or two of their visit to the phoney physicians.

ANTI-GRAVITY DEVICES

- - - -

One of the fondest dreams of many inventors has been to find a device that can neutralize gravity. Although scientists do not fully understand gravity, they do know that it is not a bipolar force. In other words, while magnets have a north and south pole—with like poles repelling and opposite poles attracting—gravity apparently exerts force in only one direction.

Device Harnesses the Forces of Gravity!

The "Dean Drive," invented by Norman Dean of Washington, D.C., in the 1950s, is basically an "anchorless winch": It converts rotating motion into motion that is directed in one direction. Dean's device received a U.S. patent, and a number of engineers actually believed that the Dean Drive could be developed into a useful machine.

Others have analyzed the tiny amount of thrust generated by the device. They have concluded that the force is present because static friction in one direction is less than it is in the opposite direction; in other words, gravity isn't really being canceled out.

Not everyone agreed with this assessment of the Dean Drive, but since the 1960s, nothing further has been heard about Norman Dean's anti-gravitational device. Some say that it didn't really work as advertised. In any case, no other anti-gravity device has ever obtained a U.S. patent.

THE DEATH RAY

- - - -

In 1924, electrical genius Nikola Tesla supposedly claimed that he invented a death ray that was capable of stopping an airplane in mid-

Electrical
genius Nikola
Tesla.

flight. Nothing more came to light until 1934, when Tesla was quoted as saying that his ray worked on an entirely new principle of physics.

Astonishing Death Ray
Stops Airplanes in Mid-Flight!

Tesla claimed that his amazing death ray was capable of destroying 10,000 planes from a distance of 250 miles. Each ray would require the construction of a $2 million plant, located at a high, strategic point. A network of twelve such death ray plants, Tesla claimed, would protect the United States from aerial invasion.

Two years later, Tesla was still trying to sell his death ray to an uninterested public; the military, too, was strangely uninterested. In the end, Tesla's invention never got off the ground, and no papers on the death ray were found after the inventor died in 1943.

FLIGHT HOAXES
- - - -

At Kitty Hawk, North Carolina, in 1903, the Wright brothers landed the first successful airplane flight. A number of previous flight attempts, however, never got off the ground. Not all were hoaxes, while others became hoaxes after the fact.

Artificial Wings
Carry Birdmen to Awesome New Heights!

One of the earliest "birdmen" was Eilmer of Malmsbury, who strapped on wings sometime around the year 1010. The early aviator supposedly flew more than 607 feet—a "stadium" in Roman measure—before crashing and breaking his legs.

In 1066 William of Malmsbury described Eilmer's feat in his *De Gestis regum Anglorum.* That leaves approximately a forty-five year gap between the event and the time it was first recorded—plenty of time to exaggerate the length of Eilmer's eleventh-century flight. Although there may not have been any conscious deception at the time, the flight of the birdman of Malmsbury is a bit too far flung to be believable.

An Italian birdman. Although the artist and inventor Leonardo da Vinci designed ornithopters (a human-powered aircraft with movable wings), parachutes, and helicopters, he apparently never used them himself. Giovanni Battista Danti (c. 1477–1517)—the other major "birdman" of the period before 1600—reportedly made several flights.

Danti's main flight—which supposedly took place in Perugia, Italy, in 1498 or 1499—was described in *Elogia Civicum Perusinorum,* written by Caesar Alesi in 1652. Danti made the wings that he wore, perfecting his technique in flights over Lake Trasimeno. During his main flight, Danti flew across the public square, where a crowd was gathered for a wedding. When one of the iron struts that controlled the left wing broke, Danti was thrown onto the roof of St. Mary's Church, injuring his leg. The written version of these "facts" did not appear until 150 years after the event, and the total distance Danti covered in his flight was not stated; it seems, however, that reports of Danti's flight have been greatly exaggerated.

Human-powered aircrafts: Even though human-powered flight is impossible, people continue to design and experiment with flying devices. The "Gossamer Condor," on the other hand, is a viable human-powered aircraft; a bicycle-pedal-powered, fixed-wing aircraft, the Gossamer Condor has successfully crossed the English Channel.

GASOLINE ADDITIVES

Many so-called inventors have claimed to have created an automobile engine that runs on water; others claim to have discovered some sort of additive that can be mixed with gasoline to fuel an automobile engine that gets hundreds of miles per gallon. The search for inexpensive fuel has led to more than a few schemes to profit from undelivered promises.

Miracle Gas from Neptune Gets Astronomical Gas Mileage!

In 1917, John Andrews demonstrated a mysterious green powder to the U.S. Navy; the powder, when mixed with water, made a fuel that ran a gasoline engine. Suspecting that they had been tricked, however, navy personnel did not follow up on the amazing gasoline powder.

Andrews produced no more inventions until 1935, when he again demonstrated the powder for the Bureau of Standards. Nothing came of the demonstration. Even so, Andrews was murdered in 1937, and the powder and his papers were stolen from his Pennsylvania home.

Secret powder and spacemen from Neptune. In 1973, Guido Franch of Chicago, Illinois, demonstrated a similar powder to automobile companies and others. Even though the powder was not available for analysis, Franch demanded millions of dollars in exchange for his invention; apparently put off by the $10-million tab, investors did not clamber to purchase Franch's secret powder.

A Pricey Lighter Fluid: In exchange for his miraculous gasoline additive, Guido Franch wanted a little financial security: He asked for $250,000 up front, with $10 million to be put into an escrow account that would become his as soon as he revealed the secret of producing the powder. On top of that, he wanted one cent for each gallon of fuel made. No one agreed to Franch's terms, and an analysis of the fuel showed that it was little more than lighter fluid.

Franch claimed that he did not make the powder, but had gotten the idea—and perhaps a supply of the powder—from a German chemist named Kraft. It seems Franch knew Kraft's mistress, who had been given a supply of the powder. He also believed that John Andrews—whom he claimed not to know—had been given some of the powder. Finally, when pressured for more answers about the gasoline additive, Franch revealed one more bit of secret information: The miracle powder, he said, came from the "Black Eagles," a group of spacemen from the planet Neptune.

You Can't
Believe
Everything
You Read

BENJAMIN FRANKLIN'S HOAXES

- - - -

Benjamin Franklin (1706–1790) had a mischievous sense of humor. Known for his wit and wisdom, Franklin was an inveterate hoaxer; most of his ruses were literary, and nearly all imparted some kind of moral lesson.

Founding Father Franklin
Fabricates Fabulous Fables!

In 1730, Franklin published a hoax in his own paper, the *Pennsylvania Gazette*. The article, titled "A Witch Trial at Mount Holly"—supposedly a news story from New Jersey—claimed that about 300 people gathered at the town of Mount Holly in order to watch a test of a man and a woman accused of witchcraft. The charge: "Making their neighbors' sheep dance ... and ... causing hogs to speak and sing Psalms." The test involved placing the accused on one pan of a large balance scale, with a large Bible placed on the other pan. Supposedly, the Bible would weigh more than a witch.

In the actual test, the "witches" each weighed much more than the Bible, but the spectators still insisted that the witch suspects be given the water test. Thrown into a pond, both suspects floated—indicating their guilt, since an innocent person was supposed to sink. The judges decided to test the suspects again—this time without their clothes—when the weather was warmer. At this point, Franklin's parody of a witchcraft trial ended.

The Gospel according to Ben. In the beginning, Franklin created a book. And Franklin said let there be an extra chapter, and there was an extra chapter. And Franklin saw the extra chapter, and it was good ... and Franklin called the extra chapter the fifty-first chapter of the First Book of Moses called Genesis.

Franklin's skills as a printer came in handy as a hoaxer. Writing with biblical flair, he added a fifty-first chapter to Genesis, creating his own ver-

sion of the Old Testament. In this chapter, Abraham offers a stranger shelter; when the stranger tells Abraham that he worships a different god, however, Abraham drives him from his house. After God appears to Abraham to tell him that he has acted incorrectly, Abraham finds the man and returns him to the hospitality of his home. People claimed that they had never seen this chapter of Genesis before; nevertheless, it *was* in Franklin's copy of the Old Testament, and it *did* sound authentic.

The slave trade and Christians in Algeria. Another of Franklin's hoaxes was a satirical attack on slavery. In a letter to the *Federal Gazette*—which had recently published an article reporting an emotional speech by a Georgia congressman urging Congress not to interfere with the slave trade—Franklin wrote that the congressman's speech reminded him of another speech. That speech, he wrote, had been delivered 100 years earlier by one Sidi Mehemet Ibrahim of Algeria.

Words of Wisdom: "Three may keep a secret, if two of them are dead." (*Poor Richard's Almanac*)

Ibrahim defended the enslavement of Christians in Algeria, claiming that it was not wrong to enslave them because they were slaves in their own countries, where despots ruled. Those who proposed to set the Christians free were misguided, he said, because the Christians were too ignorant to govern themselves; if the enslaved Christians were freed, they would raise trouble and endanger the government. The congressman's speech clearly echoed the Algerian's argument. But Franklin neglected to advise his readers of one thing: No Algerian named Ibrahim ever delivered any such speech.

Poor Richard Says the Competition Is Dead: Using the name "Poor Richard Saunders," Ben Franklin published a satirical book titled *Poor Richard's Almanac*. Spoofing astrology, he predicted the death of a rival almanac editor named Titan Leeds, pinpointing the day and even the hour of his rival's demise. When the announced time passed, Leeds vigorously denied that he was dead. Poor Richard, however, was just as stubborn in insisting that he was dead: For eight years, he swore that Titan Leeds was no more. When Leeds finally did die, Poor Richard said that the friends of Titan had finally decided to admit that their comrade had, in fact, checked into the great library in the sky.

Count Schaumbergh's letter to the Redcoats. To emphasize the evil of recruiting Hessian soldiers to fight with the British against the Americans in the Revolutionary War, Franklin wrote a spurious letter. In it, he claimed to be "Count Schaumbergh"—much like Count Schaumburg who was in charge of recruiting the Hessians. "Schaumbergh" reported that he was angry because the figures stating how many

A skilled printer, Ben Franklin created the Gospel according to Ben.

Hessians were killed in battle were understated. Since he received money for each Hessian killed, he wanted to know the correct figures in order to avoid being cheated out of any money. The British replied that the undercount was due to a number of wounded who were not counted as dead. Schaumbergh then insisted that since these men could no longer fight, the surgeons should

You Can't Believe Everything You Read

make no effort to save them. Unimpressed by the count's insouciance, British soldiers began to turn against the continued recruitment of Hessian soldiers.

Polly Baker, model mom. The Polly Baker case was possibly Ben Franklin's most influential hoax. Baker—who had five children born out of wedlock—was five times convicted of immorality. Following her last conviction, Polly appealed to the court. Her speech—reprinted many times and recounted in articles that began appearing in 1760—asked for the equal treatment of women before the law.

Polly pointed out that she supported all of her children and never turned down a proposal of marriage (the one she accepted led to her first pregnancy, at which point her husband-to-be abandoned her). She also believed that the country needed to boost its population. Finally, Polly appealed to simple math: She would be better able to support her children, she said, if the court would stop fining her for every baby born out of wedlock. She insisted that her actions hurt no one, and she also noted that no action was taken against the men in each case—each of whom was as responsible as she.

More Words of Wisdom: "But in this world nothing can be said to be certain, except death and taxes." (Letter to Jean Baptiste LeRoy, November 13, 1789)

Apparently, the story of Polly Baker struck a nerve: For years, it was republished in newspapers and magazines all over the world. But the story of Polly Baker wasn't exactly true: Franklin—who always had a moral in mind—penned the parable of Polly Baker. He seems to have modeled his story after the case of a real woman, Eleanor Kellog, who was convicted of immorality five times between 1733 and 1745, in Worcester, Massachusetts; the speech to the court, however, was strictly a Franklin fabrication.

The Silence of Ben Franklin:

Franklin's first known hoax was a series of letters published in the *New-England Courant.* In these fourteen letters--written in 1722 when Franklin was only sixteen years old--the young writer posed as a cheerful but shrewd rural widow named Silence Dogood. Dogood poked fun at drunkenness, pride, and hoop petticoats, and she favored life insurance to help support widowed women. Benjamin's brother James was the editor of the *Courant*--but there's no evidence that he knew that "Silence" was brother Ben's pen-name-in-drag.

EDGAR ALLAN POE'S HOAXES

Edgar Allan Poe (1809–1849) was best known as an American poet

-130-

Edgar Allan Poe, a well-versed hoaxer.

and short story writer. Few people have not heard of Poe's *The Fall of the House of Usher, The Murders in the Rue Morgue, The Tell-Tale Heart,* and *The Raven;* but not everyone is aware of the fact that Poe was an inveterate hoaxer, responsible for at least a half-dozen scams—some of which unfolded long after he was dead and buried.

Man Flies to Moon to Escape Creditors!

In 1835, Poe published installments of "The Unparalleled Adventures of One Hans Pfaall" in the *Southern Literary Messenger.* As the story goes, a man built a balloon and flew to the moon in order to escape his creditors. After a number of adventures, he landed at his lunar destination, spending the next five years among the moon's inhabitants. Eventually, a moon person was sent to earth with a message: Pfaall would like to return to the earth, but on two conditions. To begin with, the prodigal earthling demanded a large payment for his story; he also wanted to be forgiven for all his past crimes—including the murders of three of his creditors. Although the earth officials were willing to comply, the moon person began to fear the earthlings and left before he had their response.

Poe also planned to describe the moon and its inhabitants in great detail, but just as he was about to continue with the dubious adventures of Hans Pfaall, a British writer by the name of Richard Adams Locke completed a celebrated series of hoax articles claiming that the moon shelters "a vast population of human beings." Beaten to the punch, Poe abandoned his lunar ruse.

Ashes to Ashes, Dust to Dust:

In "The Facts in the Case of M. Valdemar," which appeared in the *American Review* in 1845, Poe claimed to have hypnotized a dying acquaintance (with his permission). As a result of this hypnosis, Valdemar appeared dead, but could still talk. This supposedly continued for several months, inspiring the unfortunate Valdemar to beg to be awakened or allowed to die. When someone attempted to awaken him, however, his body disintegrated as if he had been dead for some time. Poe's story was gruesome, to be sure, and not a little far-fetched, but many people believed it. And Poe didn't discourage them; asked whether his story was fact or fiction, he declined to comment.

"Leonainie" quoth the poet never. A poem named "Leonainie" has repeatedly been attributed to Edgar Allan Poe. Written in Poe-like handwriting and style—and signed "E.A.P."—it was supposedly found in a book in a hotel room; the writer, it seems, had left the poem in lieu of paying for his room and board.

But the poem—as a number of Poe experts testified—was definitely not the work of the author of *The Raven*. "Leonainie" was in fact a poor imitation of Poe's style penned by poet James Whitcomb Riley (1849–1916). A fair poet in his own right, Riley soon confessed that the poem was his, and even included "Leonainie" in *Armazindy,* an anthology of his poems. This did not, however, discourage others from continuing to insist that the poem was a genuine Poe piece.

Alfred R. Wallace was a stubborn man: He refused, in spite of overwhelming evidence, to admit that Poe did not

write "Leonainie." Long after the poem had been correctly attributed to Riley, Wallace received a handwritten copy from his brother in California, who claimed that the poem was Poe's. Unaware that the correct authorship of the poem had been revealed twenty years earlier, Wallace even went so far as to claim that Riley had passed Poe's work off as his own.

SHAKESPEARE HOAXES

- - - -

The author of poems, love stories, comedies, and tragedies, William Shakespeare (1564–1616) has been called the greatest writer in the English language; yet we don't know much about the man we call the Bard. And what we do know about him does not suggest that he was brilliant or educated. Because of this, many scholars have attempted to "prove" that someone other than William Shakespeare authored Shakespeare's plays.

Shakespeare "Play" Makes Bard Roll Over in His Grave!

Samuel Ireland, a retired silk weaver, was comfortably situated. He had enough money to indulge in his hobbies of rare book and curio collecting. His special interest, however, was William Shakespeare. Ireland zealously collected Shakespearean relics, and his son, William Henry (1777–1835), was eager to help. Discovering, however, that real Shakespearean items did not exist, William Henry created his own historic relics.

The audience thought that *Vortigern* was so bad that they applauded the announcement that it would not be performed again. According to one account, some of the actors' lines--notably "Oh that this solemn mockery should end"--were repeated back by the audience.

William Henry Ireland forged a number of items, including a deed with Shakespeare's name on it, a Confession of Faith by Shakespeare, and a love letter to Anne Hathaway. Although the elder Ireland was convinced of the authenticity of these items, they now appear to be clumsy forgeries.

Ireland's biggest hoax involved producing a previously unknown Shakespearean play, *Vortigern and Rowena.* After the play was "discovered," Ireland succeeded in getting Richard Brinsley Sheridan to produce it, and John Philip Kemble, a great Shakespearean actor, agreed to star in the play. *Vortigern and Rowena* was scheduled to open on April Fool's Day, 1796, but the production

was delayed until the next day. Two days before *Vortigern and Rowena* was staged, Edmund Malone, a prominent Shakespearean scholar of the time, published a book in which he denounced the play as a forgery and a hoax. Nonetheless, the performance sold out; it was so bad, however, that the play was not performed again.

Ireland never sold any of his forgeries. Since he produced them for the benefit of his father, he was never forced to answer any criminal charges. Although both father and son were at one time suspected of the forgeries, young Ireland fessed up; in 1796, he wrote a short confession as a pamphlet, followed in 1806 by a longer, book-length confession.

Forgery in the Ivory Tower. John Payne Collier (1789–1883) was a highly respected scholar, but in 1852, when experts examined an annotated copy of Shakespeare's Second Folio, they soon suspected him of fraud. Collier

William
Shakespeare.

had "discovered" the Shakespearean book—known as the Perkins Folio from the ownership inscription—in which thousands of corrections had supposedly been made in a handwriting that appeared to be contemporary with Shakespeare's. Since the First Folio printing of Shakespeare's collected works contained so many printing errors, the idea of a "corrected text"—supposedly from an authoritative hand—intrigued Shakespeare scholars.

Why did the Perkins Folio excite so much interest? The "corrector" of the text was, after all—at best—a sixteenth-century John Doe. It seems Collier himself inspired the public's interest in the inferior folio: He touted his discovery as a pivotal find, and incorporated the corrections into a new edition of Shakespeare (which sold very well).

At first, Collier never allowed the Perkins Folio to be examined out of his sight, and eventually, he refused to allow it to be examined at all. In 1858, however, Collier was forced to give in, and the staff of the British Museum examined the book. Their verdict: The Perkins Folio was a forgery and a hoax. Collier's reputation plunged, and his earlier work on the Bard was carefully scrutinized. Documents relating to Shakespeare that Collier had claimed to have discovered in the Bridgewater Library some twenty years earlier were found to be forgeries. Additionally, the manuscripts on which Collier had based

To Sign, or Not to Sign? The fact that only six authentic Shakespeare signatures are known--and little else in his handwriting--has made the Bard a prime candidate for forgers and hoaxers.

his three most famous books on Shakespeare, too, were pronounced to be bogus Bard deeds. Collier, who had access to all of the famous collections of Shakespeare materials, was accused of planting forgeries among them; he protested his innocence, but spent the last thirty years of his life in disgrace.

Dewey Ganzel reexamined the evidence in the case, and concluded that Collier was really an innocent victim. As it turns out, Collier's chief accuser was Clement Ingleby, a man who was involved in a conspiracy against the scholar. Ingleby—Ganzel says—actually knew that Collier was innocent; he was convinced that the only way to do away with the Perkins Folio's "corrections" to the Shakespeare text would be to discredit Collier completely. Ingleby, it seems, felt that the corrections were unforgivable corruptions of the Bard's perfect pearls of wisdom. Although Ganzel does make a good case for believing that Ingleby was something less than an honest man, the final verdict on John Payne Collier is still out. It's possible that Collier was, indeed, a Shakespearean hoaxer; but it's equally possible that Ingleby, or the forger of the Shakespeare text—possibly Sir Frederic Madden—were the hoaxers. In fact, it's possible that they were all involved in the scam.

Seeing Isn't

Always

Believing

FORGERIES

- - - -

Forgery is normally defined as a work of art that is presented to a buyer or audience with the intention to deceive. This fraudulent intention distinguishes forgeries from honest copies and mistaken attributions. Usually a forger paints a work in the style of a famous artist and tries to sell it, often in conjunction with an unscrupulous art dealer, claiming that it is by the hand of a famous artist. Forgers seldom try to execute exact copies of existing authentic paintings since such works are practically impossible to sell to informed buyers.

Everything You Always Wanted to Know About Forgery But Were Afraid to Ask!

As it turns out, many of the famous forgers of the past century share some common features. Forgers—most of whom are men—tend to be artists whose once-promising careers have faltered. Successful forgers often possess impressive technical skills, but, as artists, seem to have no original ideas. They use talent to imitate another artist's style; while the painting may resemble the intended work, it often lacks the inner passion and vision that animates great art.

The forger's imitative ability succeeds best where a single fake is seen in isolation. A whole gallery or portfolio of forgeries, on the other hand, is more apt to betray itself as forgery. Many forgers attempt to fake sketches and "early works" of an artist because such works can be said to have been completed before the artist established his or her mature, confident—and most recognizable—style.

There's more to forgery than meets the eye. Creating a plausible forgery is a complicated process. If a forger wishes, for example, to fake an important seventeenth-century painting, he must begin with a seventeenth-century canvas; it would be virtually impossible to create an old-looking canvas from modern materials. After finding an old—but unim-

portant—painting, the forger must either paint over the original or dissolve and scrape away the old painting.

A forgery that is painted over an old painting can be discovered if the underpainting is detected in an X-ray analysis. Trying to remove the old paint from the canvas, on the other hand, may be next to impossible, since chemicals can fuse with the fibrous material. Sometimes, forgers leave parts of the underpainting that cannot be removed, incorporating them into the design of the new forgery.

Lady Forgers: Some famous forgers have been women, such as Madame Claude Latour, who was convicted by a French court in 1947. Some of her Utrillo forgeries were said to be so accurate that even Utrillo himself couldn't be sure he hadn't painted them.

In selecting paints and brushes, the forger of a seventeenth-century painting must know the history of pigment formulas, scrupulously avoiding paints that were invented after the supposed date of composition in order to avoid revealing the fraud. For example, the color ultramarine did not come into general use until 1838, and Prussian blue does not predate 1800.

Style is all. A forger must study the brush techniques, typical subject matter, and stylistic qualities of the artist to be forged. Many forgeries are pastiche works—paintings that draw together miscellaneous elements from a number of authentic paintings in a way that fits perfectly into the established style of the older artist.

Style is, however, where even the most technically accomplished forgers usually fail. It is almost impossible for a modern painter to be able to duplicate the artistic conventions of an earlier century. Perhaps more importantly, it is next to impossible to avoid the influence of conventions and discoveries that have occurred after the work was supposed to have been painted.

A pigment of the imagination. The pigment of old paintings, acquired through time, has two characteristics: It becomes quite hard and shrinks slightly, causing a network of fine cracks (blackened with dust and dirt) called craquelure. Depending on how thick the pigment is, it may take ten years or more for a forgery in oils to dry to the hardness of an old work. Impatient to cash in on their work, forgers sometimes add solvents to their paints to increase the drying speed.

Craquelure presents a more serious problem. This effect can be mimicked by painting fine, black cracks over the surface; this technique will not, however, get past the experienced eye of a dealer or curator. The forger may try to induce cracking in the paint surface by slow baking; but even if the baked-and-cooled painting is rolled on a tube, the cracks will tend to line up in one direction, rather than extend randomly in all directions.

The forger may also attempt to achieve the effect of a cracked surface by scratching into the pigment with a needle. When the resulting surface is wiped with black ink, the result can look excellent, but the "cracks" will not extend all the way into the canvas, which may reveal the fraud. It is possible to achieve a more natural cracking by mixing egg white with pigment; this is difficult, however, because it dries faster and requires the forger to work quickly.

Once a satisfactory appearance of craquelure has been achieved, the made-to-order masterpiece requires a final varnishing. Many collectors of old art consider it a mark of authenticity when a painting is clouded by a dark varnish. Finally, a fine layer of attic dust makes the painting appear more authentic.

Every picture needs a story. When the painting is finished, the forger faces what is perhaps the most difficult task. A seventeenth-century masterpiece doesn't suddenly appear out of nowhere: There must be a believable story to explain where the painting came from and why it remained undiscovered for so long. Where was the picture hiding for the last couple of centuries? Why didn't anyone know where it was? And why is it suddenly enjoying the limelight? These aren't questions that are easily answered. First, the forger needs to invent an origin for the object. This may involve creating one or two official museum certificates with old wax seals to be affixed to the back of the canvas; a deft forger who has the skill to fake a seventeenth-century painting would have little trouble faking old certificates of authenticity.

If the forgery is of a twentieth-century work, it is sometimes possible to trick the painter's relatives—or even to exercise a little financial persuasion—to get them to sign a letter of authenticity. The forger—or the forger's dealers and partners—then need to come up with a story of how a long-lost painting happened to fall into his or her hands. Most stories are a variation on the following theme: "The old Italian family who owned this picture for generation after generation has fallen upon dire times

A Smart Investment: Although many old paintings of little value have been "recycled" by forgers, mistakes have been known to happen. One story involves a dealer who tried to sell an "eighteenth-century French" painting to industrialist Alfred duPont, claiming that it was a portrait of one of duPont's ancestors. The asking price, $25,000, eventually fell to a mere $1,000 after duPont grew suspicious. Since duPont considered the frame alone to be worth $400, he bought the portrait and showed it to a curator, who determined that the work had been altered by overpainting and suggested that the overpainting be removed. That done, the original painting turned out to be a magnificent *Madonna and Child* by the seventeenth-century Spanish painter Murillo valued then at a whopping $150,000.

and must sell the prized painting for financial reasons. The family insists on the utmost discretion—for the sake of their reputation—and must not, under any circumstances, be identified."

How much is that Picasso in the window? The price at which a forgery is offered to potential buyers is often an indication of its true status. Authentic masterpieces are never a bargain, but honest copies are cheap. Forgeries offered by fraudulent dealers tend to be priced far too high for copies, but considerably below the market value of an authentic work. How does the dealer account for this deep discount rate for a bona-fide masterpiece? The painting's owner, no doubt, has humongous debts and desperately needs immediate payment—even if it means taking a loss, as it were, on the true value of the painting.

The golden age of forgery. The nineteenth century was the heyday of forgery, when interest in classical antiquities and the Middle Ages was at an all-time high. The market for Old Masters paintings flourished, while imperial expansion created a fascination with art and craft objects from cultures beyond the "accepted" edge of civilization. Wealthy art collectors, not always quick to spot a fake, greedy dealers, and highly skilled craftsmen helped forgery to thrive as it never had. Objects that supposedly came from ancient Egypt, India, and the Far East were especially popular, as were works from medieval Europe.

The Loaves, the Fishes, and the Corot Tableaux:

Landscape artist Jean-Baptiste-Camille Corot (1796-1875) was perhaps the most forged painter in history. It's been said--in jest--that of the 3,000 or so paintings he produced in his career, about 10,000 are now in the United States. In fact, an estimated 100,000 Corot fakes are floating around the art world. Many of his paintings feature a loose, sketchy, spontaneous style that lends itself to casual forgery. Besides being an extremely popular and prolific artist, Corot was generous to the point of occasionally signing his own signature to his students' paintings. The body of work attributed to Corot is now so cluttered with fakes--some obvious and others subtle and respectable--that experts may never be able to sort out the Master from the forger.

The broad range of areas of interest inspired forgers to create new genres of art. For example, Europe was providing ivory in considerable quantities; this, combined with the popularity of medieval carvings, resulted in the creation of scores of religious carvings in ivory that supposedly dated back to the Middle Ages. Meanwhile, authentic medieval ivories lost much of their popularity among collectors because of their confusion with twentieth-century fakes.

Large numbers of forgeries of African art are currently surfacing. Workshops within Africa are producing forgeries of nineteenth-century masks, ancestral figures, and artifacts capable of fooling even the most knowledge-able experts. Since the styles of African art are many, artificial aging tech-niques are straightforward, and prices are high, the current market is rife with "old" African pieces of dubious authenticity.

TWENTIETH-CENTURY ART FORGER
- - - -

Hans van Meegeren (1889–1947), the most notorious and celebrated forg-er of the twentieth century, was born in the Dutch town of Deventer. Fas-cinated by drawing as a child, he pursued art in spite of his father's disap-proval, sometimes spending all of his pocket money on art supplies. Once in high school, he finally received professional instruction and later went on to study architecture.

Van Meegeren Earns Millions Painting Fakes!

In 1911, van Meegeren married Anna de Voogt, and the couple moved to The Hague, where the young painter received his art degree in 1914. For the next ten years, van Meegeren supported himself by giving drawing lessons and selling his own work, holding fairly well-received exhibitions in 1916 and 1922.

Van Meegeren's artistic style was essentially conservative: He painted Dutch scenes, religious paintings, the dimly lit interiors of old churches, senti-mental portraits, and works full of mysti-cal symbolism. One drawing, *Queen Juliana's Deer,* enjoyed great popularity on calendars and postcards. His political outlook was extremely conservative and bigoted, and he was opposed to all modernist tendencies in art. Although van Meegeren was successful as an artist, he began to distrust art critics, who were increasingly negative and con-descending about his work.

The artist's first forgeries. In 1923, van Meegeren divorced Anna and became involved with Johanna Oerle-mans, the estranged wife of art critic Karl de Boer. That same year, van Meegeren produced his first forgery,

Painstaking Detail: Van Meegeren used only badger hair brushes to prevent even a single modern bristle from being discovered in the paint. He also studied old pigment formulas, grinding his own lapis lazuli, for instance, to produce blue paint.

Dog or Underdog? Once van Meegeren was cheered as an underdog of the art world, his forgeries began to fetch whop-ping sums.

Laughing Cavalier, presented as the work of Frans Hals. Authenticated by an expert, the work fetched a good price at auction, but was soon detected as a forgery. Van Meegeren's involvement, however, went undetected.

Van Meegeren learned some valuable lessons from this episode, which contributed to the success of his first Vermeer forgery, *Lady and Gentleman at the Spinet.* Produced in 1932, the painting was praised as a fine Vermeer by Professor Abraham Bredius, an eminent art historian. Also that year, van Meegeren left Holland and moved with Johanna, now his second wife, to southern France.

Wifely Influence: Shortly after van Meegeren married Anna de Voogt, his artistic talents were recognized: The young artist won first prize and a gold medal from the General Sciences Section of the Delft Institute of Technology for a drawing of a church interior. Although van Meegeren agreed to sell this drawing, his wife caught him making a copy of it to sell as the original. This was the first evidence of the artist's interest in forgery, even if he was forging his own work. Although Anna van Meegeren managed to persuade her husband to abandon this petty forgery, he soon went on to paint more ambitious fakes.

For the next four years, van Meegeren supported himself by painting portraits. Meanwhile, he studied the formulas for seventeenth-century paints and experimented with ways to produce a pigment surface that had the hardness of old paint and displayed craquelure. Using volatile flower oils, he managed to perfect the technique, employing it in his greatest Vermeer forgery, *Christ and the Disciples at Emmaeus,* painted from 1936 to 1937.

A wonderful moment in the life of an art lover. Van Meegeren invented a story about an impoverished Italian family that had owned the painting for generations and did not want the family name revealed. He then set out to sell it through Dutch dealer B. A. Boon. When asked to authenticate the painting, Bredius beamed, in a 1937 issue of *Burlington Magazine,* that the discovery of Emmaeus was a "wonderful moment in the life of an art lover." He wrote:

We have here a—I am inclined to say—the masterpiece of Johannes Vermeer of Delft ... quite different from his other paintings and yet every inch a Vermeer.... In no other picture by the great Master of Delft do we find such sentiment, such a profound understanding of the Bible story—a sentiment so nobly human, expressed through the medium of the highest art.

Not everyone, however, was as enthusiastic as Professor Bredius in proclaiming the painting to be the original work of the Dutch master. In fact, having seen the painting when it was unveiled in 1937, an agent of the New York dealer Duveen Brothers wired the following cable to his bosses across the

Atlantic: "Seen today at Bank large Vermeer ... Christ's Supper at Emmaeus supposed belong private family certified by Bredius who writing article ... price pounds ninety thousand ... picture rotten fake." Fake or no fake, the painting was sold, with Bredius's authentication, to the Boymans Museum in Rotterdam, The Netherlands, for a hefty sum—equivalent today to about two million U.S. dollars. For his part, Van Meegeren received about two-thirds of the loot.

A portrait of the artist as a jailbird. At this point, van Meegeren, who now had more money than ever before, began to abuse alcohol and drugs, eventually becoming addicted to morphine. Although he had originally planned to confess his forgery to humiliate the critics who had praised the painting—and perhaps to demonstrate his contempt for critics in general—he instead forged two more Vermeer paintings.

Van Meegeren was arrested only days after the end of World War II on the serious criminal charge of having sold a Dutch National Treasure to the enemy. One of his fake Vermeers, *The Adulteress,* had ended up in the personal art collection of the Nazi Reichsmarshall Hermann Goering. Rather than face a long sentence for collaborating with the Nazis, he confessed to forgery—still a crime but not a national offense.

At first, van Meegeren's claim to have forged *Emmaeus* and *The Adulteress* as well as four other "authentic" Vermeers was greeted with more than a little disbelief. But soon there was no denying the forgery. Van Meegeren himself proposed that he paint a "new" Vermeer while he sat in jail awaiting his trial; the resulting painting, *The Young Christ Teaching in the Temple* was clearly by the same hand as the other fakes.

Van Meegeren's trial received international coverage. The artist portrayed himself as a man who simply loved to paint and whose career had been ruined by malicious critics. Having humiliated art critics—not to mention having scammed the Nazi leader who shelled out a tidy sum for the bogus opus—he became a folk hero, and the court treated him leniently. On November 12, 1947, he received the minimum sentence, one year's imprisonment. Just over one month later, however, on December 29, van Meegeren died from cardiac arrest.

A Seventeenth-Century Greta Garbo: Today it seems almost impossible to believe that the van Meegeren forgeries were mistaken for Vermeers. The faces seem strangely influenced by photography, a process that had not yet been invented. And the sentimental eyes and awkward anatomy of the figures are more reminiscent of German expressionist works of the 1920s and 1930s than of the works of Vermeer. What's more, one of the faces in Christ and the Disciples at Emmaeus bears an uncanny resemblance to Greta Garbo, the twentieth-century, Swedish-born actress.

Hans van Meegeren (seated alone in the box at left) listens to testimony at his trial for allegedly having bilked art lovers out of more than $2 million.

TWO HOAXERS: SMITH AND DE HORY

Paul Jordan Smith was the author of a number of books of fiction. He apparently disliked Picasso and a number of other artistic innovators, and, in 1924, tried to found a new school of art, the "Disumbrationist School." The next year, masquerading as a Russian named Pavel Jerdanovitch, he entered a painting in a French exhibition. Daubed in the "disumbrationist" style, the painting was called *Exaltation*. Soon, a French art journal wrote to ask for photographs of Jerdanovitch's other work. Caught in the thick of his fakery, Smith replied that he was too poor to afford photographs of his other work. Nevertheless, he did manage to provide a bogus biography of himself.

Art World Falls for Fraud and Fakery!

By now, several French art journals were praising "Jerdanovitch's" so-called disumbrationist paintings: His work looked, according to one critic, like "Gauguin, pop art, and Negro minstrelsy" combined. After three years, however, tired of his double life cum Russian artiste, Smith confessed his tale of trickery to a feature writer for the *Los Angeles Times*. On August 14, 1927, the *Times* told all about Pavel Jerdanovitch and phoney disumbrationism.

The Greatest Forger of Our Time!

Elmyr de Hory was born in Hungary in 1906. His early life is a mystery, complicated by his many pseudonyms, including Von Houry, Louis Cassou, L. E. Raynal, Hoffman, Herzog, and Dory-Bouton. There's a good chance he inherited a significant amount of money since no one ever saw him work at anything but art.

In 1946, de Hory sold one of his paintings to a woman who was convinced she was purchasing a Picasso; later, she sold the painting to a dealer as a Picasso. This gave de Hory a profitable idea: Why not forge the works of other artists? After moving to the United States, de Hory, a consummate copycat, used direct mail to sell forged Degas, Modigliani, Matisse, Renoir, and Braque paintings. In 1968, however, his scam hit a snag when a customer noticed that some of the paint was still wet on one of his paintings—a painting that should have been long dry.

De Hory later moved to the Mediterranean island of Ibiza in the Balearics. There, author Clifford Irving met him and decided to write a book about de Hory's life. We don't know whether de Hory supplied the information to Irving or whether the information came from elsewhere; we do know, however, that Irving's book is not entirely reliable. Nonetheless, the book—titled *Fake! The Story of Elmyr de Hory, The Greatest Art Forger of Our Time*—does tell of the intricate network of art dealers and middlemen who later sold de Hory's forgeries to trusting and gullible lovers of art. Someone, Irving claims, made a lot of money from de Hory's forgeries, but it probably wasn't de Hory.

Paul Jordan
Smith--founder
of the
Disumbrationist
school--was no
Gauguin.

There's No

Business Like

Show Business

BACKWARD MASKING

- - - -

Some Fundamentalist Christian ministries—notably Gary Greenwald in the beginning—have suggested that Satan prodded rock groups to record satanic messages backwards (backward masking) over the soundtracks of a number of rock albums. The messages could supposedly be heard clearly when the record or tape was played backwards, sending subliminal messages to the brain when played forward.

Satan Speaks Through Rock and Roll!

The concept of backward masking presents some questions. Assume, for the sake of argument, that some music somewhere does contain such messages. Is there any proof that people can understand, consciously or unconsciously, spoken messages that are played backwards? Obviously, if people can't understand, or even perceive, such messages, it doesn't matter much whether the messages exist or not.

In 1985, researchers Don Vokey and John Read conducted a well-controlled study in which they found that almost no one could consciously or unconsciously perceive or understand a backwards message, even one consisting of words that they already knew by heart. Therefore, even if a satanic backwards message had been recorded on an album, no one who played that message backwards would be able to understand it.

Investigators have also questioned whether ambiguous sounds can be interpreted as meaningful words, even when they are not intended as such. In 1984, researchers Throne and Himelstein demonstrated that a subject's interpretation of ambiguous stimuli is affected by what he or she expects to hear. In other words, someone warned about a satanic message on a record is more likely to find such a message than someone who has not been told to expect to hear a message.

A number of specific recordings have been accused of having satanic messages. Among the groups blacklisted by Fundamentalists are the Bea-

tles, Black Oak Arkansas, Electric Light Orchestra (ELO), Queen, Jefferson Starship, Led Zeppelin, Styx, the Eagles, the Rolling Stones, Venom, and Mötley Crüe. The backwards words supposedly include "It's better to reign in hell than to serve in heaven," "I love you said the Devil," and "Satan, move in our voices." It's possible that these so-called backwards words contain a message, but it's also possible that they're simply meaningless noises.

Some rock groups have intentionally recorded backwards lyrics as a sort of joke. For example, the group ELO has a backwards message on one of their albums that says, "The music is reversible, but time is not. Turn back, turn back, turn back." A Pink Floyd album track has this deliberate backwards message: "Congratulations! You've discovered the secret message. Please send your answer to Old Pink care of the funny farm."

Moral Muzak: In 1978, Hal Becker invented a device that inserted audio subliminal messages into music tapes. His messages--played forward--were used by department stores at a very low volume in their background music. Studies indicated that, thanks to messages such as "I am honest," and "I will not steal," shoplifting decreased in the stores where the moral sound bytes aired; we don't know, however, how controlled these studies were.

The diabolical force of Christian rock. Many Fundamentalists claim that subliminal messages are present in Christian rock songs as well. Others say that since all rock music is inspired by the devil, any subliminal messages— even the pro-Christian ones supposedly found in some songs—are demonically produced. As a matter of fact, television evangelist Jimmy Swaggart condemned "So-called Christian rock" as a "diabolical force undermining Christianity from within."

Barefoot in Heaven: At one point in the heyday of "Beatlemania," rumors of Paul McCartney's death were widespread. Part of the evidence: The *Abbey Road* album cover, where Paul alone is barefooted. The culprit: Possibly Russ Gibbs, a Detroit disk jockey, who aired the rumor on October 19, 1969.

BEATLES HOAXES

In 1964, in the early days of Beatlemania, four young men from Liverpool, Illinois, grew their hair to the then-current Beatle-length in preparation for the upcoming first series of American concerts by the Beatles. They learned to lip-synch Beatles songs, practiced British accents from movies, and convinced a friend to portray Brian Epstein, the Beatles manager; the ersatz Epstein also played Beatles music backstage.

Fake Fab Four Evades Federal Marshals!

The group started its tour in rural Illinois, but was soon playing Iowa, Montana, and other scenic spots before moving on to Boise, Idaho, and Moose Jaw, Saskatchewan, Canada. On May 24, 1964, when the *faux* Beatles were scheduled to play a gig at Rapid City, South Dakota, the real Beatles made their third live appearance on the Ed Sullivan show. Waiting at the stage door of the auditorium, federal marshals corralled the Illinois Fab Four, who were eventually forced to return their ill-gotten earnings in lieu of having to sing the jailhouse rock.

ELVIS

- - - -

Born in 1935, Elvis Aron Presley was probably his generation's most popular singer up until the time he died at the age of forty-two. Rocked by the news of the death of "the King," many Presley fans refused to believe that the legendary pop star had met an untimely end. Scores of Presley sightings, supposed photographs, and even phone calls from the dead rock star have been reported since his death in 1977.

Elvis Lives!

The circumstances of his death only helped to fuel the mystery. On August 16, 1977, Presley was found unconscious on his bathroom floor in his house—Graceland—in Memphis, Tennessee. The ambulance attendants who removed the body did not recognize Presley. Some reports say he was dead when he was found, others say he was near death. All the photographs of the death scene have disappeared from the coroner's files. Some reports say Presley was nude; others say he wore pajamas, but not everyone agrees on what color they were.

Did Elvis Know He Wouldn't Be On Tour?

Presley was scheduled to go on an extended tour the week after he died, but he didn't prepare in his usual manner. First, although Presley did go to the dentist to have his teeth cleaned the night before he died, he did not have his graying hair and sideburns dyed, as he usually did before going on tour. Also, Presley had gained so much weight that his concert costumes no longer fit, yet he didn't get measured for any new costumes for the upcoming tour.

Heart trouble—or coronary artery disease—was listed as the official cause of the death of Elvis Aron Presley. At least sixty pounds overweight in

August of 1977, Presley, who was rumored to be addicted to many prescription medications, may have died of an overdose. According to reports, the aging star took medication for high blood pressure, lupus, and glaucoma, in addition to amphetamines and tranquilizers.

Mystery surrounds autopsy. Tennessee law requires an autopsy in all cases of death where no physician or witness is present, although the results of an autopsy can be kept secret for fifty years. Such an autopsy was performed, but circumstances like these add to the mystery surrounding Presley's death:

- The coroner's office declared the case closed on the day that Presley died, before the results of the autopsy were known.

- The death certificate was issued several months after Presley's death, supposedly to replace a lost original.

- The official homicide report says the body was found unconscious. The medical examiner's report says rigor mortis had already set in when the body was found—which would mean the body had been dead for several hours.

- The contents of Presley's stomach were taken for analysis, but there is no record of any such test.

- The death certificate lists Presley's weight as 170 pounds (while some versions of the death certificate leave the weight blank). Two hundred fifty pounds would have been closer to the mark.

- A handwriting "expert" states that it is his opinion, after examining samples of Presley's handwriting, that the Medical Examiner's Report was filled out by none other than Presley himself. The medical examiner who was in charge at the time begs to differ.

Dead men don't sweat. Presley's death raised many doubts, all of which pointed to a single question: Did Presley fake his death? The singer's funeral didn't lay the question to rest: People commented that the body in the open casket didn't look exactly like Presley. A relative noticed that one of the King's sideburns seemed to be coming off. And the corpse appeared to be "sweating"; even under the sweltering Tennessee sun, dead men don't sweat.

Adding to the puzzle is an unconfirmed report that Presley's father, Vernon, acknowledged that the corpse didn't look like his son; he indicated that Presley was "Upstairs," explaining, "We had to show the fans something." What exactly was upstairs—a living fraud or a dead rock star—he didn't say.

Reports of Elvis's death: Were they greatly exaggerated? Presley is reported to have read and been impressed by the book *The Passover Plot* by Hugh Schoenfield, in which the author speculates that Jesus faked his death by taking a drug that temporarily made him appear to be dead. No stranger to medications, Presley is supposed to have been an expert on pre-

Elvis Phones Home? Sightings and photographs of Presley are ambiguous and have not been precisely dated. Friends and acquaintances of the entertainer have received phone calls from someone who claims to be Elvis Presley a living legend. Voice analysis of some of these calls reportedly indicates that the calls were made by someone who has a voice pattern nearly identical to that of Presley. Not everyone, however, believes that these results are reliable. On the "Elvis Tape," supposedly a recording of a telephone call received from Presley in 1981, "Presley" swears that he must perform in public. To date, the King has scheduled no public performance.

scription drugs. Oddly, no prescription medicines were found in his home; some people believe that his girlfriend cleaned up before calling the paramedics.

Why would Presley fake his death? One story claims that Presley—supposedly appointed as an agent of the Drug Enforcement Agency (DEA)—felt his life was threatened by individuals involved in organized crime. Presley was, indeed, issued a DEA badge: The truth is, he collected law enforcement badges. No one yet has been able to determine whether his life was in danger because of his DEA activities.

Unfinished business. Presley's life insurance money has never been collected. He was reportedly insured by Lloyd's of London—an exclusive British insurance agency that has issued policies to many entertainers—but the amount of insurance is unclear. Contributing to the loose ends surrounding Presley's legacy, an inventory of the estate left by Presley fails to list many of his personal items, such as jewelry, diaries, personal photographs of his family, and pieces of furniture.

It is possible to make a case that Presley faked his death. But there is a lot of evidence stacked against the possibility that he is alive and well and living in the nineties. The autopsy report, the fact that Presley has not performed in public, the reports of relatives who saw the body—and the difficulty of pulling off a hoax involving death—leave the burden of proof with those who say that Presley is still alive. The disappearance of key documents might indicate a conspiracy or coverup; then again, it may be the work of souvenir hunters. Did someone pay off all of the police and coroner's office employees to silence them? Speculate is about all fans can do, unless, of course, the King calls a press conference.

MILLI VANILLI

- - - -

In November 1990, the pop music world was rocked by the announcement that the album *Girl You Know It's True*—the Grammy Award-winning singing group Milli Vanilli's first album, which sold over seven million copies—had not been recorded by the illustrious twosome. Frank Farian, the German producer of the album, decided to make the hoax public when the group told him that they wanted to sing on their next album.

Farian didn't like the idea of allowing the duo to sing; he summed up his sentiments, saying "that's not really what I want to use on my records." Farian had recorded the hit song "Girl You Know It's True," which gave the album its title, before he ever met Rob Pilatus and Fab Morvan, the lead singers from Milli Vanilli. In short, it was Farian's brainchild to create the dreadlocked duo by having Pilatus and Morvan lip-synch to the lyrics of anonymous artists.

Milli Vanilli Sez
"Girl You Know It Isn't True"!

Brad Howell, Johnny Davis, and Charles Shaw aren't exactly household names. But the music they made was Top 40 fare. The National Academy of Recording Arts and Sciences awarded a Grammy to their song "Girl You Know Its True"—that is, until Milli Vanilli went down in the Hall of Shame for having lip-synched the Grammy-winning tune.

The thirty-four trustees of the National Academy of Recording Arts and Sciences, who awarded the Grammy, were furious. A telephone poll of the

Easy Come.

Easy Go.

trustees indicated that they agreed that the award should be revoked, and—before the duo had a chance to return the award—the Academy stripped them of their Grammy. The Academy also decided that the revoked Grammy would not be awarded to anyone that year.

P. T. BARNUM HOAXES

- - - -

Phineas Taylor Barnum (1810–1891) founded the circus in America. A master showman, he also authored a number of hoaxes, most of which were in good fun, and many of which were designed to raise money and generate publicity.

Circus Showman
Scammed Scores of Unsuspecting Spectators!

The exhibition of Joice Heth was one of Barnum's earliest hoaxes. In the 1830s, the father of the American circus had an agreement for the rights to exhibit Heth, who was touted as being more than 160 years old and was supposed to have been George Washington's nurse. When Joice Heth died in 1836, an autopsy was performed. The story—published in an 1836 newspaper—claimed that she was not 161 years old at the time of her death. Another story, however—in the February 27, 1836, edition of the New York *Herald*—claimed that the autopsied body was not really the body of Joice Heth; the real Heth, it seems, was still being exhibited in Connecticut.

In truth, the hoax was really on the *Herald,* which had been supplied with false information by Barnum's assistant, Levi Lyman. When confronted with his error Lyman agreed to supply the *Herald* with the real story of Joice Heth. This ran in six articles in the *Herald* beginning on September 8, 1836. As it turned out, this story, too, was a hoax. Lyman claimed that Barnum had discovered an elderly black woman on a Kentucky plantation, had her teeth extracted, taught her all about George Washington, and gradually raised her age as he exhibited her. Over a short period of time, Heth's age crept from 110 to 121, to 141, to 161 years old—a ripe old age for a southern plantation worker.

Barnum revealed in his autobiography that the story had been a figment of his assistant's fertile imagination; in actuality, Barnum had paid $1,000 for the rights to exhibit Heth for ten months. After opening an exhibit in New York City—with Lyman as the "barker"—Barnum was soon raking in a tidy $1,500 per week. It was his first success in show business. When, after a while, the New York crowds began to dwindle, Barnum took Heth on the road to tour in New England cities.

Then Heth died unexpectedly. When the autopsy report indicated that Heth could not have been more than eighty years old, Lyman planted his "wrong body" story in the *Herald,* claiming that the person who had been autopsied was an elderly woman named "Aunt Nelly." With that, Barnum's 161-year-old woman hoax expired, but not before he had reaped more than $10,000 in profits.

A diminutive general. Barnum was not above using hoaxes to promote his otherwise legitimate acts. General Tom Thumb was the name Barnum

Fish Tails and Monkey Bodies:

Barnum was also heavily involved in exhibiting fake animal composites--called Jenny Hanivers--such as mermaids made from a fish tail sewn to a monkey's upper body and head. Both of Barnum's American Museums had a number of such specimens on exhibit, and the remains of one is still on exhibit in the Barnum Museum in Bridgeport, Connecticut.

The long and short of it: P. T. Barnum and General Tom Thumb.

gave to Charles Sherwood Stratton, an American-born midget. Stratton, a Connecticut native, was not a general of any sort. One of Barnum's most successful publicity coups came when Tom married another midget, Lavinia (Minnie) Warren. Some time later, Barnum had their picture taken holding a seven-pound baby; in reality, however, the couple was childless. The child soon disappeared from the scene.

Good Sports
and
Sore Losers

ABNER DOUBLEDAY
AND THE HISTORY OF BASEBALL
- - - -

The Baseball Hall of Fame in Cooperstown, New York, honors Abner Doubleday as the man who invented the game of baseball. Few people know much about Doubleday. Fewer still know why his name has been written into the history of America's national pastime.

Baseball's Founding Father
Taken Out of the Ball Game!

Born in upstate New York in 1819, Doubleday attended West Point Academy and was commissioned into the United States Army. After serving in battles in the Mexican War, he was promoted to the rank of major by 1861. Doubleday fired the first shot from Fort Sumter against the Confederates in the attack that began the Civil War.

By 1862, he had been elevated temporarily to major general, and he played a role in several important Civil War battles, including Bull Run, Antietam, Fredricksburg, and Gettysburg. He spent the remainder of the war in Washington, D.C., and was eventually promoted to colonel after the war ended. In 1873, Colonel Doubleday retired from the service and moved to New Jersey. He died twenty years later and was buried in Arlington National Cemetery.

The special baseball commission report. A special baseball commission was set up in 1906 in order to establish whether baseball was an American invention. Charged with tracing the early history of the game, the commission of baseball experts made their report the following year. Intended as a history of the sport, it turned out to be quite a work of fiction.

Spaulding spreads the story. Sporting goods giant Albert Spaulding—one of the men who hoped to prove that baseball was as American as apple pie—relied in part on the statements of Abner Graves, an elderly

man from Denver, Colorado. Graves stated in writing that he was sure that Doubleday had invented the game as a student at Green's Select School in Cooperstown in 1839, having modified common bat-and-ball games. Graves—and the baseball commission report—claimed that Abner Doubleday, who would have been twenty years old in 1839, designed the diamond-shaped playing field, devised definite playing positions, and even thought up the name of "baseball." The story seems plausible enough, except for the fact that Doubleday was at West Point in 1839.

Rules Is Rules: When Alexander J. Cartwright formalized the rules of baseball in 1845, he drew the ninety-foot baselines and moved the batter to home plate. Cartwright also outlawed throwing the batter out by hitting him with a pitch.

Baseball—not an American game? Henry Chadwick—who was the first real baseball reporter and came to be known as "the Father of Baseball"—believed that the sport did not originate in the United States. Born in England, he claimed that he clearly remembered playing a British game known as rounders when he was a child.

Rounders had appeared in America at least a century before 1839, the year the special baseball commission claimed baseball had been invented. Chadwick believed that rounders probably derived from cricket, a bat-and-ball game that has a very long history in England. Town ball, an American version of rounders, eventually led to the game of baseball.

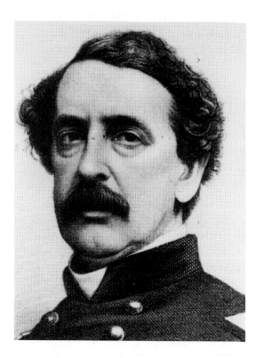

Abner Doubleday-- American as apple pie, but not the founder of baseball.

Printed rules for rounders existed in England in 1829, and rules for the game—under the name of "baseball"—can be traced back to 1834 in the United States. It looks like baseball—as we know it—was first played in New York City in 1842; rules for the game, however, were not formalized until 1845.

A deliberate hoax. Today, there is no doubt that the story that Abner Doubleday invented baseball was a deliberate hoax. Why was this West Point graduate and Civil War veteran named as the man who invented baseball? No one's telling—although some suggest that Doubleday's West Point classmate A. C. Mills, who served on the baseball commission, wanted to honor his friend. But Cooperstown is still celebrated as the place where the game was invented, and, to the general public, Doubleday retains his title as the inventor of baseball.

ROSIE RUIZ
AND THE BOSTON MARATHON
- - - -

Once a year, in April, the Boston Marathon is run over a twenty-six-mile, 385-yard foot course. The 1980 women's division winner—with the third best woman's time ever of two hours, thirty-one minutes, fifty-six seconds—was Rosie Ruiz. At race's end, Ruiz, then a twenty-six-year-old administrative assistant from New York City, was immediately crowned with the winner's wreath.

Fleet-Footed Rosie Ruiz Races to Fishy Finale!

No sooner had Rosie donned the winner's wreath than skeptics began to question her victory. Why hadn't anyone seen her among the leaders of the race during the critical period before the final mile? How could Ruiz run so fast in Boston when—six months earlier—she had finished *663rd,* in twenty-fourth place among the women, in the New York Marathon? And why didn't Rosie look tired after her twenty-six-mile stroll through Beantown?

The evidence was mounting, and Ruiz wasn't smelling like a rose. Several witnesses insisted that they had seen Jacqueline Gareau—the second-place finisher—leading the women all along, with Patti Lyons in second place. Several sportscasters who were commenting on the race for radio and TV also said they had not seen Ruiz near the front of the pack, if they saw her at all. And two runners assigned by WGBH-TV in Boston to watch for the lead man and woman at the halfway point both said they never saw Rosie Ruiz. Nonetheless, several witnesses did say they had seen Ruiz at the twenty-five-mile point in the women's lead and at other points in the race.

Runner-up: Jacqueline Gareau of Montreal, Canada, the 203rd person to finish the race, was the second woman to cross the finish line in the 1980 Boston Marathon. She claimed that the first time she saw Rosie Ruiz was when she saw her--after race's end--crowned with the winner's laurels.

The virtues of public transportation. Although Ruiz said that she would be willing to take a lie detector test, she never did. And Rosie's athletic history was beginning to rewrite itself. A woman by the name of Susan Morrow came forward to say that she had met Rosie Ruiz on the subway in New

York City—*during* the 1979 New York City Marathon. She said she had ridden with Ruiz—who was wearing a contestant's uniform—from the ten-mile point of the race to Columbus Circle, near the finish; she also said she walked with Ruiz to the finish line. Ruiz, it seems, had qualified for the Boston Marathon based on a race she never finished.

Rosie misses roll call. Ruiz denied ever having met Morrow, but the evidence continued to stack against her. Officials of the Boston Marathon, who had compiled five lists of runners in the lead during the first twenty-four miles, pointed out that Rosie Ruiz's name did not appear on any of the lists. Finally, two Harvard students settled the Beantown disagreement: It seems they had seen Ruiz jump back into the race less than a mile from the finish. A seven-day intensive investigation and the review of more than 10,000 photographs of the race failed to show Rosie Ruiz at any point before the final

Rosie Ruiz's
fifteen minutes
of fame.

mile. In the end—stripped of her New York Marathon time and deposed from her Boston crown—Rosie Ruiz lost more than a foot race.

THE CASE OF SIDD FINCH
- - - -

Sportswriter George Plimpton told the story of Hayden (Sidd) Finch in the April 1, 1985, issue of *Sports Illustrated*. Finch, it seems, was a baseball pitcher who was able to throw a fastball at 168 miles per hour. During spring training at the New York Mets camp in St. Petersburg, Florida, the six-foot-four, twenty-eight year old was considered a pitching prodigy.

Phoney Finch winding up for the pitch.

Brawny Brit Fires Fabulous Fastball!

Although Finch was from England, he had perfected his fastball during several years of practice in Tibet. His father, an archaeologist, had been killed in a plane crash in Nepal. After dropping out of Harvard after one semester, Finch was spotted by Mets scout Bob Schaefer in Maine, where Finch was playing for the Mets' AAA Farm Club. Schaefer, dumbfounded by the speed and accuracy of Finch's fastball, invited him to appear at the St. Petersburg spring training camp. Finch insisted on secrecy and several other conditions, and the Mets agreed.

Scams Illustrated. Plimpton's article was heavily illustrated with photos of Finch and Mets players and trainers taken in St. Petersburg. Readers—especially sports writers—were, in a word, intrigued. Plimpton, it seems, had decided, along with Mark Mulvoy, the editor of *Sports Illustrated,* to publish the magazine's first April Fool's article. Plimpton came up with the subject, the real Mets agreed to allow photographs to be taken at their spring training camp in St. Petersburg, and the fabulous Finch was played by a friend of the photographer; although his real name was not recorded, some people believe that he was a school teacher from Chicago.

A Pitcher, a Yogi, an April Fool's Joke. Plimpton's article was so well written that there was scarcely a clue that it was a hoax. Almost no one had noticed that the first letter of each word in the introduction of the original article spelled a secret message: "He's a pitcher, part yogi and part recluse. Impressively liberated from our opulent life-style, Sidd's deciding about yoga and his future in baseball." The message was: "H-A-P-P-Y-A-P-R-I-L-F-O-O-L-S-D-A-Y."

Sports Illustrated finally unveiled the hoax after having received a deluge of phone calls about Finch from readers. The April 8 issue of *SI* reported that Finch had lost his pinpoint accuracy; following a press conference, the prodigious pitcher simply waved to the crowd and walked away from baseball forever.

VICTOR NOTARO'S SOCCER STORIES

- - - -

In March 1982, thousands of Canadians were thrilled to read about an Ontario teenager who led the Canadian junior soccer team to victory in a World Cup championship in Sydney, Australia. Victor Notaro was that teenager, and the whole story was an elaborate hoax.

Canadian Teenager
Seeks Sports Trophy--the World Cup!

Notaro began by sending information from Kalamazoo, Michigan—where he attended college—to his hometown newspaper in Canada. The material included information about the upcoming tournament in February, and Notaro's role on the Canadian team that would be playing in Australia. Canada beat West Germany, Brazil, and the Soviet Union—all with the hoaxer's help—and Notaro provided telephone reports of each victory to the local newspaper, Ontario's *Welland Tribune*. After the *Tribune* passed the information on to the Canadian Press Agency, newspapers all over Canada picked up the news of the spectacular success of the Canadian soccer team.

Soon, however, some of the other papers checked into the story and found that the tournament did not exist. Confronted by reporters, Notaro admitted that he made up the story; he was just a hometown boy looking for a local sports trophy.

Heroes,
Bad Guys, and
Impostors

ABRAHAM LINCOLN HOAXES
- - - -

Abraham Lincoln, whose presidency lasted from 1861 to 1865, has been indirectly involved in a number of hoaxes. His signature and documents have been widely forged, and words that he never spoke have been written into history through phoney speeches and quotes.

History Put Words in President Lincoln's Mouth!

The Bixby letter was supposedly written by Lincoln to a widow who lost five sons in the Civil War. However, experts say that Lincoln did not actually write the letter, the original of which has never been found. The president's secretary, John Hay—an expert in imitating Lincoln's handwriting—probably wrote the letter to the grieving mother. What's more, it seems that the writer of the letter was mistaken about how many sons Bixby had lost: Bixby lost two—not five—sons in the Civil War.

In 1928 and 1929, the *Atlantic Monthly* magazine mistakenly published a collection of phoney Lincoln papers when it printed love letters that Lincoln supposedly wrote to Ann Rutledge. Reading between the lines, Lincoln scholars dismissed the letters as fakes, and the magazine discontinued publishing the phoney presidential love notes.

Words the president never spoke. During the 1880s, a number of Lincoln speeches were published—speeches that contained material never written or even uttered by President Lincoln. For instance, he supposedly said:

I see in the near future a crisis that unnerves me, and causes me to tremble for the safety of my country. As a result of war, corporations have been enthroned and an era of corruption in high places will follow, and the money power of the country will endeavor to prolong its reign by working upon the prejudices of the people until all the wealth is aggregated in a few hands and the republic is destroyed.

This was the last picture ever taken of Abraham Lincoln. The glass negative cracked during developing, and the photographer never got a second chance to pose the president: Honest Abe was assassinated the following week.

The trouble is, Lincoln never said this. Other made-up quotes have been used to suggest that Lincoln favored a high tariff and that he favored Italian unification, an issue he never actually addressed.

In 1896, *McClure's Magazine* published what it called "Lincoln's Lost Speech." Since no one had written down the speech, which was supposedly delivered at the Republican State Convention in Bloomington, Illinois, in 1856, experts believed that the original text had been lost. In 1930, after carefully studying the speech that appeared in McClure's, Lincoln scholars concluded that it was a fake. The original text of "Lincoln's Lost Speech" has never been found.

DICK TUCK'S HOAXES

- - - -

D ick Tuck pulled off a number of hoaxes in the realm of politics, but he is best known for his pranks on Richard Nixon. Some were hoaxes, others were simply pranks, but all were at the expense of the thirty-seventh president of the United States.

Political Prankster
Preys on "Tricky Dick" Nixon!

Charged with setting up a college rally to introduce Nixon, Tuck obtained a 4,000-seat auditorium. He knew, however, that only a small group would attend; a total of forty people entered the 4,000-seat auditorium. Before Nixon began, Tuck announced that he was going to wait for more people to show up. None did; instead, ten people left.

Attempting to stall the proceedings, Tuck asked Nixon all sorts of questions—under the guise of "introducing" the politician. Finally, he said "Richard Nixon will now speak on the World Monetary Fund." Nixon, who had never intended to speak on the World Monetary Fund, was at first stunned and speechless.

Garbage trucks and a kiss on the cheek. When Nixon was running with Dwight

Plagued by prankster Dick Tuck, Richard Nixon's sense of humor was put to the test.

D. Eisenhower for reelection as vice president, the Republican Convention was held in San Francisco. Tuck discovered that the main route taken by many garbage trucks going to the city dump passed right by the convention center. This inspired him to use the dump trucks to advertise his opinion of the vice president: Each truck bore the slogan, "Dump Nixon."

During the 1960 Nixon/Kennedy race, Tuck orchestrated yet another incident. As Nixon descended from an airplane the day after his first debate with John F. Kennedy, a woman—sent by Tuck—approached him. She kissed Nixon on the cheek and said, "That's all right, Mr. Nixon. He beat you last night, but you'll win next time." A bit unsettled, Nixon eventually managed to compose himself.

An action-packed speech. Dick Tuck denies having authored the hoax that most people think was his best ever—although he claims he wishes he had masterminded the prank. As the story goes, Richard Nixon was delivering a speech from the rear platform of a train. Someone dressed in a conductor's uniform motioned at the train, which left the station—while Nixon was still talking. Tuck denies having had anything to do with the incident. In fact, the prank is not documented, and actually may never have happened.

HITLER SURVIVED WORLD WAR II

- - - -

As the Russians advanced within Berlin, Germany, on April 30, 1945, Germany's führer Adolf Hitler was in his bunker under the Reich's Chancellery with several other people. Among those present were Nazis Joseph Goebbels and Martin Bormann; Eva Braun, Hitler's mistress; two of Hitler's secretaries; Erich Kampka, Hitler's chauffeur; Hitler's servant Heinz Linge; and several guards. Hitler was in poor health: his hands trembled severely, perhaps due to Parkinson's disease, perhaps because he chronically abused amphetamines. After the Russians overran Berlin, the Kremlin announced Hitler's death on May 2; some thought the Russians had ulterior motives in proclaiming Hitler dead.

Adolf Hitler Is Alive and Well!

In its May 2 announcement, the Russian news service Tass stated that the Germans had reported that Hitler had died at noon the previous day, and he had named Admiral Doenitz to succeed him as chancellor. The Tass statement added that "by spreading the news of Hitler's death, the German Fascists apparently wish to give Hitler the means of leaving the stage and going underground." Stories of Hitler's escape spread like wildfire. Some said that he and Nazi officer Bormann had escaped from Germany by taking a submarine to South America; others said Hitler was alive and well and living in Antarctica.

Hitler's henchmen. Some of Hitler's deputies—such as Josef Mengele and Karl Eichmann—did manage to escape. Mengele was never captured. Eichmann, however, was captured in Argentina, convicted, and executed in Israel for war crimes. Martin Bormann also escaped, but was apparently captured and killed shortly thereafter; his skull was identified in 1972.

Bodies in the garden. The Russians delayed releasing the autopsy report on Hitler's body for more than twenty years—which only fueled rumors about Hitler's escape. The report did not surface until 1968, when

it appeared—buried—in a Russian book by a former Soviet intelligence officer by the name of Lev Bezymensky. The book claimed that Russian counterintelligence (SMERSH) had captured the guard who witnessed the bodies of Hitler and Eva Braun being taken from the bunker to the garden and burned. SMERSH discovered the bodies of Joseph Goebbels and his wife, and, on May 4, 1945, dug up the bodies of a male and female who had been buried in the garden outside of the bunker.

At first, the agents did not believe that the remains were the bodies of Hitler and Eva Braun, but a careful search of the bunker did not produce their bodies. When the guard who witnessed the burning later added that he was present when the burned bodies were placed in a bomb crater and covered with dirt, SMERSH carefully examined the exhumed bodies.

The autopsy report: The teeth tell all. The autopsy report of the two bodies buried in the garden said that both died after they had bitten into cyanide capsules: Glass fragments had been found in the mouths of both corpses. The male body had also been shot in the head—after he had taken the poison. And, like Hitler, the man had only one testicle.

Dental records provided proof positive that the body in the garden was that of the infamous Nazi leader. Using the remains of the body's extensive dental work, the Soviets matched Hitler's teeth with records from his dentist's office. Eva Braun's body, too, was identified by her dental work.

Dead men don't travel. Reporters hoped to question Bezymensky about his book, but the Soviets allowed no such meeting. The Soviets also claimed that Hitler had requested Heinz Linge, his servant, to shoot him after he swallowed the poison capsule, but Linge denied having shot Hitler. In fact, Linge and another witness both claimed that Hitler had not taken poison, but had shot himself.

Clearly, Hitler did not escape. But that hasn't stopped people from claiming to have "sighted" him in nearly every country of the world since the end of World War II. What's more—putting aside the question of whether or not Hitler died in his bunker—he would now be well over 100 years old if he were still alive.

JACK THE RIPPER HOAXES
- - - -

At least five women died at the hands of a single murderer in London in 1888; the killer, however, was never publicly identified and may never have been caught. Over the years, a number of books and articles have claimed to solve the killings and reveal the identity of the killer. The murders, committed by a man known as Jack the Ripper, were no hoax; but the quest to find out who he was and why he savagely murdered his victims has inspired more than a few wild stories.

Five Women Die Gruesome Deaths at Hands of Ripper--Whoever He Was!

Although some people attribute eighteen murders to the Ripper, only five can be definitely attributed to the same killer. The first killing was that of forty-three-year-old Mary Ann Nichols, on August 31, 1888. The body was found on Buck's Row (now Durward Street) in Whitechapel, then a dangerous slum area of London's East End. As a matter of fact, Whitechapel was where all the murders took place. Nichols, a prostitute, had her throat cut, as did all the victims; Nichols's corpse also had several deep slashes in the abdomen.

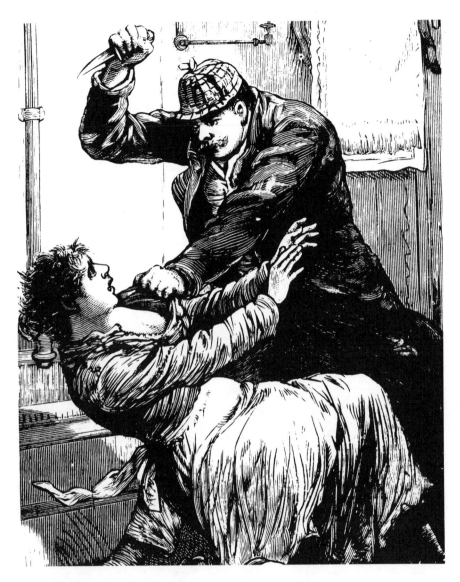

The London killer might have called himself "Jack the Ripper," but the name itself may be a hoax.

Annie Chapman, the second victim, a forty-seven-year-old prostitute, was found murdered on September 8, on Hanbury Street. Chapman's body had been terribly mutilated: Her intestines had been strewn about and her uterus had been removed. On September 30, the third victim, prostitute Elizabeth Stride ("Long Liz") was discovered with her throat cut, although her body was otherwise unmutilated; the authorities believed that her killer was interrupted

before he could mutilate her. Catharine Eddowes ("Katie Kelly"), age forty-six, was also killed that night in Mitre Square; she, too, was a prostitute. Eddowes was severely mutilated and cut about the face; her uterus and one kidney were removed.

By this time, the news agencies and police had received several infamous letters signed "Jack the Ripper." The writer of the letters boasted that he would not be caught and that, after cutting off the ears of one of his victims, he would send them to the police. A later letter enclosed a piece of human kidney, although it can't be determined whether it was the one removed from Eddowes.

The final and most horrific murder occurred inside the room where prostitute Mary Jane Kelly lived. On November 9, the body of Kelly, who was about 25, was found in her bed; the body was horribly mutilated. This was to be Jack the Ripper's last killing. Some people believe that the killer suddenly died; others believe he was secretly captured and committed to an insane asylum; and others speculate that the Ripper quit after he had eliminated all of his intended victims.

The queen, a baby girl, and blackmail. Author Stephen Knight proposed a "solution" to the murders, but he had no facts to bolster his theory; in fact, his main witness admitted that his story was pure fiction. Knight believed that all five of the victims knew each other: They were specific targets of the killer, who was trying to dispose of them because they were blackmailing the queen.

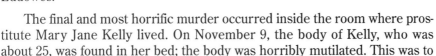

The Long List of Suspects: Many men have been named as the infamous Jack the Ripper over the past century, including Druitt, a mentally ill barrister; Gull, a royal physician; "Leather Apron"--possibly John Pizer--a butcher; Stephenson, a mad poet; Stanley, the father of a man who caught syphilis from a prostitute; Pedachenko or Ostrog, a Russian physician; Eddy, the Duke of Clarence, a royal grandson; Cream, a mentally ill surgeon; and Kosminski, a man who despised prostitutes.

According to Knight's story, Queen Victoria's grandson, Prince Edward Albert, who was second in line for the throne, secretly married a Catholic girl and had a baby girl with her. This child, who would be third in line for the throne, was a Catholic (by birth) and would have destroyed the entire Anglican basis of the monarchy if she ever became queen. The Home Secretary, therefore, issued the order to kidnap the woman and kill the child.

Supposedly, the five murdered women had witnessed the kidnapping and were attempting to blackmail the queen. According to Knight's theory, three men acted as the murderers: Sir William Gull, the Queen's physician; John Netley, the Queen's coachman; and Robert Anderson, an assistant commissioner of the Metropolitan Police. It would have been easy to lure a prostitute

into a royal coach, and, since the murders were committed inside a royal coach, there were no witnesses. The bodies, in turn, were dumped in an alley.

Gull committed the murders, making them look like the work of a madman who was seeking revenge for a personal betrayal. What's more, Gull's involvement ties in a chalk inscription that was found on a wall near one of the killings. The inscription—"The Juwes are the men that will not be blamed for nothing"—had previously been taken as an illiterate reference to "Jews"; Knight, however, notes that "the Juwes" referred to a high Masonic official, known to the upper ranks of the Freemasons. As it turns out, Gull was a Freemason.

This story, supposedly told to Knight by the son of artist Walter Sickert, has a lot going for it. But it doesn't hold up under close investigation. For instance, there were two laws that prevented the throne of England from ever being occupied by a Catholic. According to The Royal Marriages Act, any secret marriage of the royal family could be set aside as invalid if the royal family member was under the age of twenty-five or had married without the queen's consent; Eddy, not yet in his mid-twenties, had definitely tied the knot without grand-mama's official blessing. And the Act of Settlement of 1700 minces no words in excluding any person who married a Roman Catholic from inheriting the crown. Between these two laws, the motivation for the entire plot crumbles. In any case, Walter Sickert's son Joseph admitted that the whole story was a fraud.

A portrait of a Ripper? Sir William Gull.

Visions of murder. Robert J. Lees (1848–1931), a spiritual medium, offered another hoax to explain the Jack the Ripper murders. On April 28, 1895, the Chicago *Sunday Times and Herald* ran a story claiming that Lees had a vision of one of the killings before it occurred. Lees apparently had approached the police, but they quickly dismissed him as a quack. The following night, however, a murder occurred exactly where, when, and how Lees had described it; the police were suddenly more interested in what the psychic had to say.

The next time Lees went to the police with another vision,

·25· Sept· 1888.

Dear Boss.

I keep on hearing the police have caught me but they wont fix me just yet. I have laughed when they look so clever and talk about being on the right track. That joke about Leather apron gave me real fits. I am down on whores and I shant quit ripping them till I do get buckled. Grand work the last job was. I gave the lady no time to squeal. How can they catch me now. I love my work and want to start again. You will soon hear of me with my funny little games. I saved some of the proper red stuff in a ginger beer bottle over the last job to write with but it went thick like glue and I cant use it. Red ink is fit enough I hope ha. ha. The next job I do I shall clip the ladys ears off and send to the police officers just for jolly wouldnt you. Keep this letter back till I do a bit more work. then give it out straight. My knife's so nice and sharp I want to get to work right away if I get a chance. Good luck.

yours truly
Jack the Ripper

Dont mind me giving the trade name

Written in red ink and signed "Yours truly, Jack the Ripper," this letter was addressed to the "Boss" at the Central News Office in London.

he told them that the killer would cut off the ears of his victim. The police were particularly interested since they had just received the letter—signed "Jack the Ripper." Lees supposedly accompanied the police to the scene of the next Ripper killing and received an impression of the killer that allowed him to trace the murderer back to his house.

The home was that of a prominent physician; although the physician has not been named, Gull, once again, is regarded as the suspect. After a bit of cajoling, the doctor's wife agreed to speak to the police; what she told them didn't paint a flattering picture of her husband. The doctor, it seems, had a strange character flaw: he flew into rages and sometimes behaved sadistically. Judged before a panel of his peers, he was declared insane and committed to an asylum, where he died shortly thereafter.

Lees's story, too, has a number of problems. To begin with, the police deny that any of this happened—and their files don't indicate otherwise. Furthermore, Gull was neither judged insane nor committed; in fact, a thorough search failed to find such records for any London physician who had been committed to an asylum. Apparently, Edwin T. Woodhall, a British journalist, was responsible for spreading this Ripper tale. Woodhall reworked the original 1895 Chicago newspaper article in the 1930s, and, accepted as true, the article was eventually reprinted in many books and magazines.

The Ripper remains anonymous. Many other suspects have been identified as Jack the Ripper, but it is unlikely that the bloody truth will ever come to light. Many people hoped that the London files, sealed for a century, would offer the final solution. Once opened, however, the files simply listed the usual suspects, with no real proof to identify the killer.

Ripper aftermath. After the murders, Prince Eddy's wife was supposedly confined to a mental asylum, where she died. As for the baby girl—whose birth set in motion the spate of murder and blackmail—no one knows what happened to her. An intensive search, however, produced no record of a marriage of Prince Eddy or of the birth of a child to the woman he supposedly married. The woman, named Ann Elizabeth Crook, was real, but she never married Prince Eddy. The Prince died quite young from what was probably influenza, although he might have died from paresis, or syphilis of the brain.

The Last Attack: The Ripper's final victim, Mary Jane Kelly, was killed indoors. According to Stephen Knight's scenario, another Mary Kelly (also known as Katie Kelly) was accidentally killed when she was mistaken for Mary Jane Kelly. When the killer or killers realized their mistake, they tracked down Mary Jane Kelly and killed her at home. With her death, all of the queen's blackmailers were dead.

FERDINAND WALDO DEMARA

- - - -

Ferdinand Waldo Demara (1922–1982) has been called "The Great Impostor"—and rightfully so. He successfully impersonated many individuals including a surgeon, psychologist, college dean, dentist, professor, and a Trappist monk.

Impostor Bamboozles
Surgeons, Monks, and Navy Brass!

Demara grew up in Lawrence, Massachusetts. Running away from home at the age of sixteen, he joined a Trappist monastery, where—put off by the monks' asceticism—he stayed for only two years. Demara then enlisted in the U.S. Army, and, assigned to Kessler Field in Biloxi, Mississippi, he realized almost immediately that he had made a mistake.

Demara discovered that the orderlies who rounded up recruits for transfer to other units seemed to avoid the worst duties. Soon, he masqueraded as an orderly, complete with fake armband and clipboard; what's more, he seemed to know exactly what he was doing. In short, Demara had taken his first step toward a life as an impostor.

Good credentials: The key to imposture. As a young soldier, Ferdinand Demara was invited to the home of a fellow soldier. The soldier's proud mother showed Demara her son's many diplomas and certificates; Demara was inspired. Returning to the soldier's house, he made off with enough material to create a new identity for himself as that soldier.

Twice Trappist and the art of teaching science. Having assumed the identity of his fellow soldier, Demara was admitted to another monastery. All went well—for a while—until a student from the first monastery recognized Demara from his former monastery. After only one week, Demara fled, eventually enlisting in the U.S. Navy. Just after the bombing of Pearl Harbor, he was sent to Hospital School, where he received first aid training.

Demara, now interested in the medical field, applied for advanced training. When he was turned down on the grounds that he did not have enough education, he managed to obtain the credentials of one Dr. Robert Linton French, a psychologist. Using French's credentials, Demara secured a teaching position in science at a boy's school run by a Catholic order. Staying just one lesson ahead of his pupils, Demara managed to keep his scam afloat until the abbot checked his credentials. Fired, he stole the abbot's car and headed for Chicago.

Fake papers, a war crime and eighteen months in the slammer. Once in Chicago, Demara started training for the priesthood, but he left when it looked like he'd have to go through another rigorous training period that included self-denial. Using his psychology "credentials," Demara became dean of the School of Philosophy at Gannon College in Erie, Pennsylvania. But his grand schemes for improving the college—and his position there—soon led to his dismissal.

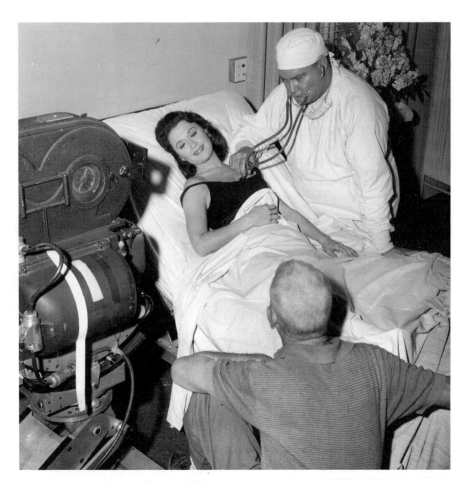

The great impostor, Fred Demara, playing doctor in *The Hypnotic Eye*, a United Artists movie.

Demara then traveled to an abbey in Washington, where he successfully ran a student psychological counseling center. Appointed as deputy sheriff, Demara was again undone by a background check that turned up his criminal past. Arrested and led away in handcuffs, Demara was charged with deserting the navy in wartime, a capital crime. In spite of his memorable self-defense, the Great Impostor served eighteen months in prison.

A growing academic career. Freed from prison, Demara immediately enrolled as a law student in Boston. As soon as he completed his first year of law school he left for Maine, where he became a biology professor at a small college. After helping to turn the small college into a university, he left in a fit of anger when he was informed that he would not be promoted at the new university. But he didn't leave empty-handed; before quitting those hallowed halls, Demara managed to procure copies of the credentials of Joseph Cyr, the physician who treated some of the faculty.

Fifteen minutes of fame ... and then some. Having sold his story to *Life* magazine, Demara committed a $2,500 mistake. The general public, now familiar with Demara's face and checkered background, was no longer easily duped. Appointed as a prison officer under the name Ben W. Jones, Demara soon became warden of the maximum security block at the Huntsville, Texas, jail. When a prisoner saw the article in *Life,* Demara's prison career came to an abrupt end.

Returning to Maine, Demara ran a local school—until he was arrested yet again. When the local townspeople rallied to his defense, praising his abilities as a teacher, the charges were dropped and Demara left town.

The end of a brilliant career. Demara's career as an impostor suffered a final blow when Robert Crichton's book *The Great Impostor* appeared in 1959; the book was later made into a movie starring Tony Curtis. It became all but impossible to continue the masquerade, and Demara was forced to get by on his own name.

The New Dr. Cyr Gets in Trouble:

The "new" Dr. Joseph Cyr enlisted in the Royal Canadian Navy as a surgeon lieutenant. For six months, he bluffed his way through diagnoses and treatments without ever losing a patient; he even performed a number of difficult operations successfully. While in Korea, the ersatz doctor removed a bullet near one patient's heart, and he removed another patient's bullet-pierced lung. A story about the good "doctor's" medical triumphs was published--against his wishes-- and Demara's past caught up with him again; the real Dr. Cyr had read the story and realized that someone had borrowed his background. Demara was dismissed from the navy for entering under false pretenses. But the navy never raised the more serious charge-- of practicing medicine without a license--in order to avoid charges that it had provided improper care.

After moving to California, he worked in various youth counseling positions. Twice charged with child molestation, he was successfully defended by attorney Melvin Belli. Demara worked in his final position—as a visiting counselor at Good Samaritan Hospital in Anaheim, California—until illness forced him to retire. Demara died at the age of sixty on June 8, 1982.

MARTIN GUERRE

– – – –

The case of Martin Guerre (born in 1525) is one of the most famous and complex cases of imposture. The basic story is simple. A woman named Bertrande de Rols Guerre and her husband Martin Guerre lived in the village of Artigat in southern France. In 1553, after nearly ten years of marriage, Martin Guerre disappeared.

French Impostor Sentenced to Hang!

Four years later, a man claiming to be Monsieur Guerre appeared in the village. He looked something like Martin and he knew a lot about Bertrande—and about Martin's past life. If he wasn't the real Martin Guerre, he had studied his subject well. Bertrande accepted him as her husband, and within the three years they lived together, they had two children. Many people accepted this man as the real Martin, and when others expressed their doubts to Bertrande, she reassured them that he was, indeed, the real Martin Guerre.

Martin Guerre and *Sommersby:* The French movie *Le Retour de Martin Guerre* (1981) is based on this case. Although the film is basically accurate, some historians continue to dispute certain aspects of the case--for example, whether Martin's wife, Bertrande, was involved in the ruse. The movie *Sommersby* (1993), starring Richard Gere and Jody Foster, is a remake of *Le Retour.* The plots are very similar, except in *Sommersby,* the hoax takes place just after the Civil War.

Curiosity kills the impostor. When Martin began asking his wife's relatives about how much property she owned and what it was worth, he aroused more than a little suspicion; her relatives informed the authorities that something was amiss. The new Guerre (whose real name was Arnaud du Tilh) was arrested and brought to trial for adultery and imposture. Convicted, du Tilh was sentenced to death by hanging—although he insisted to the bitter end that he was Bertrande's legitimate husband.

During the trial, the long-absent original Martin Guerre returned to the village. Having lost a leg in battle, he was nonetheless easily recognized—and accepted—by Bertrande, her family, and the rest of the villagers. The court, although suspicious of the war veteran for having deserted his family, decided not to prosecute him.

A possible accomplice. The court also had to decide whether Bertrande was consciously aware of du Tilh's deception and whether she had willingly participated in adultery. After a lengthy deliberation, the judges decided that Bertrande had, indeed, been deceived—for more than three years—by a man who pretended to be her husband. Still, the court's reasoning seemed more like a pardon than a verdict of innocence. In fact, the court ordered Bertrande to pardon her husband and to reconcile with him since she had been so easily led into fraud by the bogus Martin Guerre.

BRUSHY BILL AND BILLY THE KID

- - - -

A number of impostors claimed that the notorious outlaw Billy didn't die as a kid; among them was a Texan by the name of Ollie L. "Brushy Bill" Roberts.

Billy the Kid Grows Up!

Supposedly, the twenty-two-year-old Kid—whose real name was William Bonney—escaped the trap set for him by Sheriff Pat Garrett at Fort Sumner, New Mexico, and lived to a ripe old age as "Brushy Bill." Skeptics pointed out, however, that Roberts had also claimed to be Frank James (the brother of Jesse James). Using authenticated photographs of the Kid and "Brushy Bill" to compare twenty-five facial "landmarks," experts determined, by computer analysis, that the two men were clearly different individuals. As author Gregory Byrne has said, "It seems bad guys, or at least their legends, don't want to die."

Rebel without a cause--Billy the Kid.

Orlando Scott a Chicago, Illinois, doctor stands with the mummy that toured sideshows as the body of John Wilkes Booth.

JOHN WILKES BOOTH

- - - -

Many people believe that President Lincoln's assassin, John Wilkes Booth, was not the man who was shot in a Virginia barn on April 14, 1865. Over the following decades, some forty men have "confessed" to being the infamous assassin.

Former Actor Gets Top Billing at Carnival Sideshows!

One such confessor, known as David E. George, committed suicide at Enid, Oklahoma, in 1903. Finis Bates, a shrewd lawyer from Memphis, Tennessee, obtained George's long-unclaimed but remarkably embalmed body. Identifying the body as John St. Helen, Bates claimed that the dead man had earlier confessed his true identity to him. Bates published this "true" story in *The Escape and Suicide of John Wilkes Booth,* and for years, the mummy of "Booth" was exhibited at carnival sideshows. The mummy superficially resembled the actor-turned-assassin, and it even had fractures and wounds similar to Booth's. Nevertheless, when Michigan's *Dearborn Independent* investigated the mummy in 1910, it debunked the sideshow spectacle as a fraud.

ANASTASIA AND ANNA ANDERSON
- - - -

In the summer of 1918, the immediate Romanoff family was supposedly shot to death in the cellar of a house in Ekaterinburg. Years later, Anna Anderson—having been fished out of a German canal by the police—claimed that *she* was in fact Anastasia, the sole surviving daughter of the Romanoff Czar Nicholas II. Her story was convoluted but not entirely implausible: Anastasia *could* have survived, had she been shielded from the assassins' bullets by her sister's dead body. On the other hand, if Princess Anastasia did expire with the rest of the Romanovs, then Anna Anderson is clearly a counterfeit countess.

Romanoff Princess Escapes Assassination!

In 1920, three years after the Romanoff shooting, the police pulled a bedraggled woman from a Berlin canal. The woman, who had tried to kill herself, was taken to the hospital with no money or identification papers. The next day, she was transferred to the Dalldorf Psychiatric Hospital, where three psychiatrists claimed she was in a deep depression that probably affected her memory.

Weeks later, another inmate read an article about the murder of the Romanoff Czar. Included was a picture of the late Czarina, which prompted the patient to notice Anastasia's uncanny resemblance to a mysterious inmate whose identity was unknown. When hospital doctors learned of the resem-

blance, they contacted one of the former Czarina's ladies-in-waiting who lived in Berlin at the time. The woman visited the nameless inmate at the hospital and announced that there was no doubt: the patient was indeed the ill-fated Princess Anastasia.

The woman who rose again. Suddenly, the mystery woman's memory began to improve. Anna Anderson—as she later called herself for privacy—remembered falling down when her family was shot in the basement. The next thing she remembered, she woke up in a cart driven by two soldiers. For a number of days, the cart wound through country backroads, and Anna overheard the soldiers mention that they had crossed the Romanian frontier. The soldiers, brothers Alexander and Serge Tschaikovsky, were Red Guards who had been present at the execution. Although they were anti-Czarists, they were still loyal to the Czar; when they saw that Anastasia was still alive, they wrapped her in a blanket and placed her in a cart rather than the truck that was bound for the burial site.

Moles and Scars and Memory Lapses:

Anna Anderson shared a number of characteristics with Anastasia, the heir to the Romanoff fortune. She had bunions, a small scar on her right shoulder from the removal of a mole, a scar on the left hand middle finger, and one on the forehead (both of which were from childhood accidents). On the other hand, she couldn't speak a word of Russian--a fickle forgetfulness for a Romanoff princess. Although at least a dozen Romanoff relatives agreed that Anna was indeed Anastasia, several others--including her Swiss tutor and her godmother--dismissed her as a fraud.

Troubled times for Mrs. T. In Romania, Anastasia married Alexander—which explains why Anna Anderson often called herself "Mrs. Tschiakovsky." She had one child, but within a year, her husband was mysteriously murdered on the street. After placing the baby in an orphanage, she moved to Germany with her brother-in-law, living from the sale of jewels she had stitched inside her undergarments. One day, however, her brother-in-law went out, never to return. After searching for him for hours—and having sold the last of her jewelry cache—she impulsively threw herself into the canal. For seven years after Anastasia was "discovered," she checked in and out of nursing homes, recovering from the after-effects of her traumatic experiences.

Princess or Peasant Girl?

In 1927, a private detective claimed that Anna was really a peasant girl named Franziska Senanzkovsky who had disappeared in Berlin three days before Anna was found in the canal. Although Franziska's landlady identified her, Anna stuck to her story and left for the United States. There, she stayed with her cousin, Princess Xenia, who hadn't seen Anastasia since they were children. Princess Xenia was convinced that Anna was her long-lost cousin: After all, she remembered where and when they had played together as children.

Returning to Europe, Anna Anderson filed a series of lawsuits attempting to collect her late father's fortune. Finally, in 1967, the German courts rendered their final verdict: All of Anna's claims to the royal booty were rejected. Having retired in Germany's Black Forest while her claims were pending, the 67 year-old Anna married John Manahan, an American history professor. She lived with him in Charlottesville, Virginia until she died in 1984—insisting, even as an octogenarian, that she was Romanoff royalty.

Skeletons in the Closet!

Not everyone believed that Princess Anastasia escaped the assassins. In 1992, in a front-page article in the London *Sunday Times,* Paul Bahn and Tim Rayment reported that the graves of Czar Nicholas II and his family had been opened. Eleven bodies were found near the assassination site at Ekaterinburg—which corroborates reports of the investigation of the killings in 1919. Among the skeletons found at the Russian burial site was one identified as Anastasia; pierced by a bayonet wound, her body was found just outside the pit holding the nine other bodies, along with that of her sister Tatiana.

Archeologists believed that the Romanoff daughters were still alive after the shooting, having been protected from the bullets by the jewelry they'd hidden in their underclothes. The girls—whose parents had been shot to death—were stabbed by bayonets and left by the side of the pit where the rest of their family was buried. As previous reports had claimed, the bodies were stripped and burned, doused with acid, and hidden, and the ground above the site was crushed under the wheels of a heavy truck. In short, it doesn't look like Anastasia escaped from Ekaterinburg that fateful summer day in 1918; recent forensic studies—in which the DNA in Anastasia's hair samples were compared to the bone DNA from the skeleton—show that Anna Anderson was *not* related to the Romanoffs.

DAVID HAMPTON

— — — —

In 1983, a young African American man who claimed to be David Poitier, the son of actor Sidney Poitier, conned his way into the homes of a number of prominent New Yorkers. Introducing himself as a friend of one of their children, he finagled invitations to their posh Manhattan digs by feigning tem-

porary impecunity. It wasn't long, however, before David Hampton—the ersatz actor's given name—made headlines for posing as a Poitier.

Fifth Avenue Wannabe
Scams Unsuspecting Socialites!

Buffalo, New York, was no place for boy wonder. "There was no one who was glamorous or fabulous or outrageously talented there," David Hampton once lamented in *People* magazine. "I mean, here I was, this fabulous child of fifteen, speaking three languages, and they didn't know how to deal with me." The eldest of three children, Hampton attended a string of prestigious high schools—never to graduate from any.

Fifteen Minutes of Fame: When David Hampton appeared at Andy Warhol's office posing as the son of Sidney Poitier and Diahann Carroll, Warhol had him thrown out. Having overheard that the artist was planning to dine with Halston later that evening, Hampton waltzed into the designer's home claiming that the pop art czar was expecting him. Halston, too, expelled the bogus Poitier. Hampton's efforts, however, did not go unnoticed: He's mentioned in three entries in *The Andy Warhol Diaries.*

Beckoned to the big city by bright lights and pipe dreams, the aspiring *artiste* left his upper-middle-class family to try his luck in New York City. Once ensconced in the city—in a friend's quarters—the seventeen-year-old Hampton supported himself by working odd jobs at a bookstore and an ice-cream parlor—with more than a little clandestine financial support from his mother. Having earned a state high-school-equivalency diploma, Hampton returned to Buffalo the following year, where he bounced from one college to another (managing nonetheless to earn a rap sheet in California). Twice arrested at SUNY Buffalo, he was banned from campus (eventually serving a six-month prison sentence for criminal trespass). Soon, Hampton was anathema at Columbia University, too, where he was accused of stealing from dorm rooms, having gained students' confidence by claiming to be the friend of a gay-rights leader.

They call me Mr. Poitier. There was one thing of which David Hampton, the son of a prominent Buffalo attorney, was sure: He wasn't leading the life of luxury he so richly deserved. Then, one night, having been refused entry to New York's glitzy Studio 54, he experienced an epiphany. Posing as the son of Sidney Poitier, Hampton and his friend—the "son" of Gregory Peck—suddenly found that doors flung open for them. "We were swept in like we owned the place," Hampton told *People.* "It was sort of a magical moment."

And one good magical moment deserved another. At Connecticut College, Hampton, *cum* David Poitier, soon became a big man on campus, casting extras for a film his father was directing. When Hampton left Connecticut, he took with him the address book of Robert Stammers, a student he'd met at the college. Stammers says Hampton stole the book from him; Hampton, on the other hand, doesn't see it that way. All quibbling aside, the book was a Park Avenue wannabe's dream come true, brimming with the names and addresses of Stammers's schoolmates at Andover.

Guess Who's Coming to Dinner!

Jay Iselin, now president of Cooper Union, and his wife, Lea, an attorney, had a daughter who attended Andover with Stammers. On September 30, 1983, using the address book, Hampton telephoned the Iselins, introducing himself as David Poitier, a friend of their daughter's and a student at Harvard. He claimed to be down on his luck: Having arrived in town to meet his father—who was due to fly in from the West Coast to start rehearsals for a film version of *Dreamgirls*—he had been mugged, and therefore needed somewhere to spend the weekend. The Iselins were glad to oblige; inviting him to spend the night, they fed him and gave him pocket money. When they were awakened in the middle of the night by scuffling noises, however, they became suspicious. The next morning, Hampton, who claimed to have chased a burglar from their home, begrudgingly left, at the Iselins' request.

Two days later, Hampton phoned Osborn Elliott, then dean of Columbia University's Graduate School of Journalism, and his wife, Inger, with the same story, this time claiming to be a friend of the Elliotts' daughter. The Elliotts, too, opened their doors to Hampton: They paid his cab fare, included him in a dinner party with a South African friend who was staying with them, gave him $50, and invited him to stay overnight. And they, too, soon regretted their generosity. When Inger Elliott went into David's room the next morning to wake him up, she was surprised to find a second houseguest. Hampton assured the Elliotts that the man in bed with him was in fact Malcom Forbes's nephew; nevertheless, they asked him to leave. Oz Elliot also asked Hampton to return the $50, but the young man claimed already to have spent it on flowers for the missus.

After learning that the Iselins had been duped by Hampton, Inger Elliott called the police. The Police Department's special fraud squad discovered that the Elliotts and the Iselins were in good company: David Poitier, it seems, had preyed on the kindness of at least eleven other people, including a Manhattan urologist and a young actor and his wife, who had given Hampton $350. The fraud squad also discovered that David Hampton was a celebrity in his own right: Charges against him included grand and petit larceny, illegal entry, failure to pay for service, invalid use of a credit card, and resisting arrest.

Heroes, Bad Guys, and Impostors

Six Degrees of Incarceration!

Sentenced by a State Supreme Court judge, Hampton was ordered to repay the whopping $4,500 he had taken from his various hosts. Failure to comply, the judge warned him, would result in prison; on January 10, 1985, Hampton entered Dannemora state prison. A contrite con man he was not. "Basically the individuals involved here that I took for a ride," Hampton later explained to *New York* magazine, "in a way it serves them correct that they were taken for a ride because they have clustered themselves into this little world and sheltered themselves from the realities of New York City. This is the very reason that Saddam Hussein invaded Kuwait."

Wasting no time behind bars, Hampton dialed some familiar phone numbers. He was going to write a book about his story, he informed his erstwhile victims, and, if they sent him money, he'd be sure to portray them favorably. Released on October 6, 1986, Hampton soon picked up where he'd left off; three months later, he was arrested in a Buffalo suburb for criminal impersonation and fraudulently obtaining transportation.

Stupid Is As Stupid Does:

Soon after having added New York University to his list of forbidden campuses, Hampton was arrested and charged with theft of services, menacing, and criminal possession of a weapon. It seems he refused to pay a cabdriver while brandishing something that looked like a gun. He then missed his court appearance, later claiming that he had been in an accident en route to the courthouse; he even produced a report from the ambulance company that supposedly took him to the hospital. Pleading guilty to stiffing the cabbie, Hampton received three years' probation, less than a week of community service, and a $500 fine. He walked out of court a free man--that is, until he was slapped with a warrant for possession of a bogus document (the forged ambulance report).

Hampton Seeks the Spoils!

Six years after Oz and Inger Elliott told him about their encounter with Hampton, playwright John Guare picked up a copy of Sidney Poitier's autobiography. In May 1990, *Six Degrees of Separation* opened at the Mitzi E. Newhouse Theater at Lincoln Center to rave reviews. Meanwhile, more than a little peeved that he wasn't sharing in the spoils, David Hampton threatened to sue Guare, and when First Amendment specialists didn't see things his way, he tried to extort money from the playwright. "I'm going to become totally, totally vicious," Hampton told *New York* magazine in March, 1991. In May, 1991, a criminal court judge ordered Hampton to stay away from Guare, who complained of threats against his life. Denying such threats, Hampton admitted to having had "a few acrimonious conversations" with his pseudo-biographer. Guare's attorney, it turns out, had taped recordings of these acrimonious exchanges: "I would truly advise you to give me some money," Hampton advises Guare on the tape, "or you can start counting your days."

Having given up on posing as a Poitier, Hampton was determined to benefit from the success of Guare's play. At New York University, posing as a graduate student who had written *Six Degrees of Separation*—which hadn't yet been made into the hit movie starring rap artist Will Smith—he claimed to be negotiating a movie deal with Spike Lee. Within a month, having worn out his welcome, Hampton added NYU to the list of campuses from which he'd been banished. Since then, Hampton—who "would rather be known for positive achievements than as a slickster in an off-Broadway play"—has complained of having trouble with a person impersonating him. Michael Donohue, an associate business manager at Playwrights Horizons, claimed that someone identifying himself as David Hampton earned a few meals, a place to sleep, and eventually the ill will of his host by posing as the *leading man* in *Six Degrees of Separation.* Donohue wanted to press charges, but the police said their hands were tied: they couldn't charge David Hampton for impersonating David Hampton.

WILLIAM DOUGLAS STREET, JR.

- - - -

In 1971, Detroit native William Douglas Street, Jr., headed south and donned a Tigers uniform, hoping to strike it big in the major league. Although a failure on the baseball diamond, he was a gifted impostor; posing as a surgeon, a lawyer, a student, and a journalist, he conned his way through operations, depositions, exams, and interviews before landing a four-and-a-half- to ten-year sentence for forgery in 1984.

Chameleon Fumbles Baseball Tryout!

Doug Street—who came to be known as the latter-day "Great Impostor"—decided early in life that he didn't want to follow in his father's footsteps. A Detroit bus driver, William Douglas Street, Sr., worked double-time as a male nurse to make sure that his wife and five children were well provided for. Long on talent but short on patience, Doug Jr., armed only with a high school diploma, set out to prove that he was as good as—if not better than—the athletes and professionals he saw on TV.

Convinced that only a lack of opportunity stood between him and the baseball Hall of Fame, Street plotted a shortcut to the pitcher's mound. In February, 1971, posing as Jerry Levias, a wide receiver for the Houston Oil-

ers' football team, who happened to have played second base in college, Street contacted Hoot Evers—an erstwhile outfielder who was at the time in charge of Detroit's farm teams. Claiming to be at odds with the Oilers and fed up with football, Street conned an airline ticket to the Tigers' spring training camp in Florida. "That was the first time I found out how easy it was to get people to believe whatever you said, as long as you said it right," he later boasted.

The Big Squeeze: Encouraged by having talked his way into a Tiger uniform, Street decided to try another scam. Less than a month after having been booted from training camp, he dropped by the Detroit home of Tiger outfielder Willie Horton--who, Street knew, was still in pre-season training in Florida. Having delivered an extortion letter to Mrs. Horton--in which he threatened the outfielder's family--he expected to collect the $20,000 he demanded. What he didn't count on was the fact that he was no stranger to Mrs. Horton, who had seen a picture of him in a Tiger uniform and remembered him as a first-class passenger en route to the Sunshine State only weeks earlier. Street's next role was that of a contrite would-be extortionist, played in the chambers of Recorder's Court Judge John Murphy; given the choice between a year of prison with two years' parole or no time with twenty years' probation, he opted to stay out of prison. The road to Kinross prison, however, is paved with good intentions.

The trouble was, he *didn't* say everything right: When Street, *cum* Levias, boasted that he'd make it to the A-team before year's end, reporters were eager to find out whether the Oilers shared his sentiments. It seems they didn't. What's more, Street, who—at five feet, ten inches, and 175 pounds—talked a good game, he lacked the speed and accuracy of a professional athlete; in fact, he didn't even *look* like an athlete. After fumbling some grounders in front of the increasingly skeptical scouts, Street finally threw in his glove, and walked away with no contract—and no lawsuit. Gypped out of the price of a plane ticket, and more than a little embarrassed, the Tigers' management let Street walk away scot-free and $300 richer, thanks to a loan from Gates Brown.

Impostor Hoaxes Hospital!

After a brief and unsuccessful bid as an All Star football player, Street skipped parole and moved to the Windy City, this time posing as a doctor at Illinois Masonic Hospital. During his three-month internship, Street—who substituted a Harvard Med School sheepskin for his Central High diploma—assisted in some sixteen surgical procedures, including hemorrhoid operations, mastectomies, and stomach resectionings. "Most people wouldn't want to hear how easy it is," he later claimed; on that count, he's probably right.

When Street's medical career was cut short after a routine security check revealed that his social security number matched that of a known parolee, his career moved behind bars. Then, trading his lab coat and stethoscope for a three-piece suit and attaché, Street decided to take a sabbatical from prison and landed a legal position with the Detroit Human Rights Department. Having been trained in prison as a legal researcher, he was made for the part. In an office rented in a Detroit law firm, with a Cornell diploma displayed for all to see, Street reviewed civil rights law and recommended action for citizens who submitted complaints. None of his superiors questioned why a law-school graduate student who was working for free would spend forty-hour weeks behind a desk in Detroit. Less than three months later, however, they were bursting with questions when the police, acting on a tip from Street's estranged wife, hauled him away.

I Think, Therefore I Scam!

After another stint behind bars—during which time he studied college-level economics and psychology—Street set his sights a little lower, this time posing as a student at the University of Michigan Law School. But not just *any*

law student: Wearing a naval officer's uniform to class, Street boasted of his achievements at Annapolis, claiming to have been in the running for a Rhodes scholarship. Eager to recruit the young officer, a Detroit lawyer ran a background check on his would-be associate, only to discover that Street's legal expertise was, in a word, unorthodox. In the spring of 1989, the lawyer informed university officials of Street's ruse.

Undaunted by the warrant issued for his arrest—for a $600 "misunderstanding" involving a classmate's check—Street took his tax final, which he failed, before skipping off to New Haven, Connecticut. Four months later, while attempting to register at the Yale University Medical School with a fake student I.D., Street found himself enrolled in the New Haven City Jail, where he spent a brief retreat before being returned to Kinross prison in Michigan. Paroled in 1989, he kept a low profile for a couple of years. In late 1994,

The Wright Stuff: Posing as a *Time* magazine writer who was in Boston to write a piece on Red Sox player Carl Yastrzemski, Street convinced club officials that he needed a Red Sox uniform "just to get the feel of it." Ousted for warming up in the bullpen during a game, Street later found the uniform to be a handy prop for pulling scams as a minor league "prospect"; appearing on a Detroit television talk show, for instance, Street collected $50 for posing as a ballplayer. "We should have been suspicious," a spokesperson for the Boston Red Sox rued, "of a writer who writes to us saying that he wants to 'wright' about our ball club."

however, he was jailed on two counts of obtaining money under false pretenses and possessing another person's credit card. Investigating his involvement in the fraud, police discovered that chameleon Street had been up to his old tricks: Using a social worker's certificate he'd obtained with false documents, William Douglas Street collected $38,000 in fees by posing as a certified social worker at a Troy, Michigan clinic.

No barrel of laughs. To date, Street has spent about twenty years in prison, most of it for parole violations. His latest conviction—for credit card fraud for having racked up some $10,000 in charges against his girlfriend's credit cards—inspired a Michigan judge to sentence him to six times the recommended sentence in order to "protect the community." "Reporters call me up and they think this is all fun, a barrel of laughs, fooling everybody," Street once lamented. "But people don't like to get fooled. They keep putting me in jail and I keep wondering why I keep on doing it when it isn't getting me there and it isn't even fun."

Chameleon Street, Wendell B. Harris Jr.'s 1989 film about the mercurial Mr. Street, won top prize at the prestigious Sundance US Film Festival in 1990.

AIMEE SEMPLE MCPHERSON'S KIDNAPPING

- - - -

Aimée Semple McPherson (1890–1944) was a popular American evangelist in the 1920s and 1930s. In 1926, at the peak of her fame, she suddenly disappeared. According to newspaper reports, she had been swimming in the Pacific Ocean off Los Angeles, California, when she vanished; five weeks later, in the desert of Mexico, she suddenly reappeared.

Woman Evangelist Vanishes to Romantic Seaside Resort!

On May 18, 1926, McPherson invited her mother, Minnie Kennedy, to accompany her to the beach. When her mother declined, McPherson went instead with her secretary, Emma Schaffer. After seeing McPherson far out in the water, Schaffer eventually lost track of her boss. Later, when McPherson did not return to shore, Schaffer spread the word that she had drowned.

An extensive search, however, produced no body. The newspapers were teeming with questions and reported sightings of the evangelist in small California towns. The police, meanwhile, had received a number of ransom demands, but they remained skeptical about McPherson's disappearance. Nonetheless, Kennedy offered a $25,000 reward for the return of her daughter alive.

Five weeks after the disappearance, the Los Angeles police received a call that McPherson had surfaced in Douglas, Arizona. A little while later, the errant evangelist phoned home. Kennedy warned her daughter not to speak to anyone about her "kidnapping." By the time her mother arrived in Arizona, however, McPherson had fraternized freely with the paparazzi.

Aimée claimed to have been abducted and tortured after having been lured to a car parked by the beach by someone who told her a story about a dying infant. Once inside the car, she was overcome by chloroform. When she awoke, she was bound to a cot—somewhere in northern Mexico.

Her escape could have taught James Bond a thing or two: She rolled off the cot, cut her bonds with a discarded tin can, and finally managed to climb out a window. She then walked through miles of desert to the Mexican border town of Agua Prieta, just across from Douglas, where she collapsed.

Justice Paid Is Justice Delayed:

Although it was not revealed until much later, the judge in McPherson's case, Carlos Hardy, accepted a check for $2,500 from the Angelus Temple, McPherson's church organization. Several years later, Hardy was tried at an impeachment hearing for having accepted the check and for other unprofessional conduct. At that hearing, the memory of many of the witnesses from the kidnapping case several years earlier seemed to improve. Suddenly, they were all able to identify McPherson as the mystery woman who had been with Ormiston at the seaside cottage. Hardy, it seems, had instructed some of the witnesses to be certain of their identification.

An unlikely story. Not surprisingly, not everyone lent a sympathetic ear. The press, in particular, questioned her story: After all, how—after dragging through miles of scorching desert heat—could Aimée emerge without sunburn or injury? And she wasn't even thirsty. What's more, her clothing wasn't torn, and there were grass stains on her shoes.

Word began to spread that Kenneth Ormiston, McPherson's radio station engineer, had been seen with her at a seaside resort during the time in question. Ormiston and the evangelist had been linked romantically before, and his wife had threatened to name McPherson as the reason she was seeking a divorce from her husband. Apparently, Kennedy ended the scandal by forcing Ormiston out of his job; after he had left the area, she then paid him to come back to Los Angeles during a time when it was rumored that he was traveling in Europe with McPherson.

McPherson claimed that her kidnappers had cut off some of her hair to send to her mother, along with a demand for a $500,000 ransom. Kennedy did receive an envelope containing a lock of hair, along with a demand for that amount of money; if the ransom was not paid, the note said, McPherson would be sold into white slavery in Mexico. The police questioned the note's authenticity.

Both Aimée McPherson and Minnie Kennedy were called before a Los Angeles grand jury formed to investigate the incident. The grand jury found

Aimee Semple McPherson.

enough evidence to try them for "conspiracy to perpetuate a hoax," and
Kennedy was arrested for obstruction of justice. During the days leading up to
the trial, much money changed hands in order to influence key players in the
case. At the eleventh hour, the district attorney decided that no one would be
well served by a trial, and he dropped all charges. The public, however, did not
forget.

AMBROSE BIERCE AND RELATED DISAPPEARANCE TALES

- - - -

Ambrose Bierce (1842–1913) was known in literary circles as a wit, cynic, journalist, and writer of horror stories. He is also known for having vanished in 1913, never to be found again. A veteran hoaxer, Bierce probably orchestrated his own mysterious disappearance—but investigators will never know for sure. What they do know is that Bierce's stories inspired more than a few bizarre—and suspicious—tales of inexplicable disappearances.

Writer Vanishes Without Trace!

Bierce was a very persuasive writer. In *Can Such Things Be?* he convinced many readers that his accounts were authentic, or at least based on true events. But research indicates otherwise; in fact, the author himself wrote, "With a hardy mendacity that I now blush to remember I gave names, dates and places with a minute particularity which seemed to authenticate the narratives that I came near to a belief in some of them myself." On one occasion, Bierce cowrote a book, *The Dance of Death,* in which he pretended to condemn the waltz as "shameless." Then, using a phoney name, he wrote a column that discredited and panned the book.

He Blinded Them with Science: In "Science to the Front," Bierce relates the crackpot theories of "Dr. Hern of Leipsic." Hern, a product of Bierce's imagination, had a theory: "In the visible world there are void places," he claimed, rather like "cells in Swiss cheese." These cheese-like void places, it seems, are somehow responsible for mysterious disappearances. Hern's cheese theory, not surprisingly, didn't cut it with the scientific poobahs.

The end of a pleasant correspondence. There is plenty of evidence to suggest that "the Old Trickster," as Bierce was known, planned his own disappearance. In fact, Bierce once wrote an essay supporting suicide as a way to avoid debilitating old age; he also told his publisher that he owned a German revolver for just such a purpose. Bierce selected a location in the Colorado River gorge where his corpse would be protected from vultures. In farewell letters to his friends, he made dramatic statements such as, "This is to say good-by at the end of a pleasant correspondence," and, "My work is finished, and so am I." Bierce also wrote to his daughter to give up his cemetery plot: "I do not wish to lie there," he wrote, "That matter is all arranged and you will not be bothered about the mortal part of [signed] Your Daddy."

Bierce made it look as though he was traveling to Mexico, possibly to serve with the bandit revolutionary leader Pancho Villa. After he disappeared, supposedly after leaving Chihuahua, Mexico, the American consul investigated; there was no evidence, however, that Bierce had ever been there. Privately, the Old Trickster confessed, "You need not believe all that these newspapers say of me and my purposes. I had to tell them something." He also vowed in a letter, "And nobody will find my bones"; no one ever has.

Lang: A Faint Voice Crying for Help!

David Lang walked into his pasture on September 23, 1880, and—in full view of his wife, children, and a family friend—vanished. The shocked onlookers immediately ran to the spot where he was last seen, but no trace of the

Wordsmith Bierce was lampooned in the early 1890s.

Tennessee farmer remained. No hole or any other clue offered an explanation of the mysterious disappearance. As time passed, a circle of stunted grass marked the spot where Lang was last seen; sometimes, from within the circle, family members heard his voice faintly calling for help.

Again, historical research fails to substantiate the story. In fact, there was no evidence of any farmer named Lang. There is, however, a first-person account by Sarah Emma Lang, who claimed to be David Lang's daughter. Her account, "How Lost Was My Father?," appeared in the July 1953 issue of *Fate* magazine. The story turned out to be a hoax. Nevertheless, Lang claimed to communicate with her father through "automatic writing."

The story of David Lang, like the stories of Oliver Larch, was inspired by Ambrose Bierce's trilogy; in this case, the source was "The Difficulty of Crossing a Field," which describes the witnessed vanishing of an Alabama planter named Williamson.

THE BERMUDA TRIANGLE
- - - -

V incent Gaddis coined the term "Bermuda Triangle" in 1964 to describe an area in the Atlantic Ocean roughly bound by Puerto Rico, the Bahamas, and the tip of Florida. Gaddis—a self-made "researcher" who promoted the "mystery" of spontaneous human combustion—suggested that the Bermuda Triangle spelled doom for all who ventured into its domain, and other writers since Gaddis have continued to sensationalize the story. Inspired by the disappearance of several dozen ships and planes in "the Devil's triangle," scads of writers have speculated about "time warps," UFO kidnappings, and other equally bizarre "theories."

"Mysteries" of the Sea: According to the U.S. Coast Guard, even when the vanishings actually occur within the Triangle, "there is nothing mysterious about disappearances in this particular section of the ocean. Weather conditions, equipment failure, and human error, not something from the supernatural, are what have caused these tragedies."

Devil's Triangle Decimates
Teams of Tankers and Torpedo Bombers!

On the clear and sunny afternoon of December 5, 1945, Flight 19, a group of Avenger torpedo bombers, vanished. The five bombers left Fort Lauderdale Naval Air Station for a routine two-hour patrol; instead, after a few brief radio exchanges with other planes and ground receivers, all five planes disap-

Flight 19--a group of Avenger torpedo bombers like these--vanished into thin air on December 5, 1945.

peared. Headed for the last estimated position of Flight 19, a giant Martin Mariner plane with a crew of thirteen also vanished; no trace of any of the six planes has ever been found.

Nevertheless, in *The Bermuda Triangle Mystery—Solved,* reference librarian Lawrence David Kusche concluded that the so-called triangle was "a man-

ufactured mystery." Citing a Navy investigation's report on the fate of Flight 19, Kusche showed that the patrol was made up of rookies; what's more, their leader was obviously disoriented and had changed direction a number of times during the four hours the squadron was lost. And other factors—such as the approach of bad weather, poor radio reception, a failed teletype, and a military rule that required the planes to stay together—contributed to the squadron's desperate situation.

Kusche believes that the planes ran out of gas and were forced to ditch at sea during a stormy night. "Had any one of these factors not prevailed," he says, "the flight might have ended differently. One or more of the planes might have made it back, and the event would have been forgotten, rather than becoming known as the strangest flight in the history of aviation."

As for the Martin Mariner, its disappearance is no real mystery: Dubbed "flying gas tanks" because of the dangerous fumes that were often present in

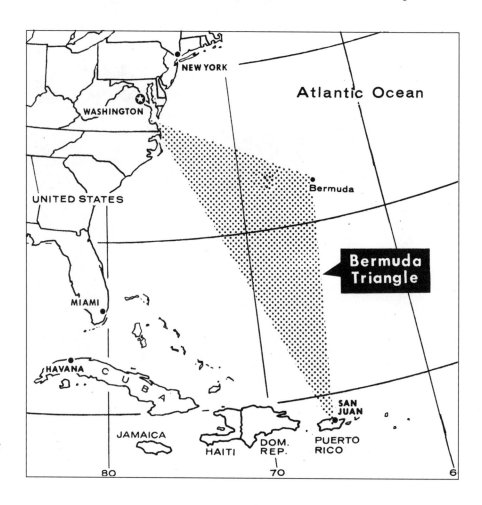

Some say the Bermuda Triangle is really more of an oval or a trapezoid.

the fuselage, the planes sometimes burst into flames when a spark or a crew member's cigarette ignited the fumes. And, contrary to popular belief, the Mariner was not the only plane that searched for the lost patrol: Other planes left both before and after the Mariner, and returned unscathed.

Public Mystery Number One Debunked. Kusche has debunked a number of Bermuda Triangle "mysteries." For example, an abandoned ship was found drifting off the Florida coast in 1944; the puzzle fell in place when a hurricane—omitted from most writers' accounts—was restored to the scenario. A plane that allegedly vanished in the Triangle in 1950 actually exploded in 1951, some 600 miles west of Ireland. And yet another plane, a British troop transport that disappeared in 1953 "north of the Bermuda Triangle" probably crashed in torrential rain and wind some *900 miles* north of the Triangle.

A life preserver (tied to a man's shirt) and a life jacket--stenciled with the words "S.S. *Marine Sulphur Queen*"--were surrounded by sharks when they were plucked from the Atlantic Ocean.

Kusche summed up the situation thus: "Previous writers, either on purpose or because they were gullible, created the mystery. I found that many things writers call mysterious really aren't if you take the trouble to dig for some information. Previous writers on this topic had to be either very poor researchers with little curiosity, very gullible, or outright sensationalists. They've been passing off their own lack of information as mysteries."

The Sulphur Queen Vanishes

The S.S. *Marine Sulphur Queen* supposedly vanished in the Triangle in early February 1963. The tanker, en route from Beaumont, Texas, was last heard from at 1:25 A.M. on February 4, as it neared the Straits of Florida. On February 9, when it was one day overdue at Norfolk, Virginia, the *Sulphur Queen* became the focus of an air and sea search. Over the following days, the search was widened, but no corpses, lifeboats, or oil slicks provided any clue as to the tanker's mysterious disappearance.

Eventually, some wreckage surfaced, proving that the vessel did not simply vanish: Patrollers found a piece of an oar and other debris from the tanker, including a name board that bore the letters "ARINE SULPH" between its shattered ends. The fact that the tanker did not send a distress message suggests that whatever happened happened suddenly. The vessel was structurally weak, plagued by fires, and probably encountered rough weather. With a cargo of 15,260 tons of molten sulphur, the ship might have exploded—as did a similar vessel carrying liquid benzene in 1972—or it might simply have sunk in deep water.

Witchcraft on the Atlantic!

Still another touted Triangle mystery occurred in December 1967, when a twenty-three-foot cabin cruiser named *Witchcraft* disappeared with its two-man crew just off Miami Beach. The men reported a damaged propeller to the Coast Guard and asked to be towed back to port. They also reported that the boat's hull was intact and that the built-in floatation chambers rendered the craft virtually unsinkable. Yet, when the Coast Guard reached the location—after only nineteen minutes had passed—there was no trace of the boat, the men, or their life preservers. It looked like the infamous Triangle had claimed two more victims.

In truth—contrary to the way the incident is usually portrayed—the craft was disabled in rough weather amid six-foot waves. Without the use of its engine propeller to steer in the waves, the boat could easily have been swamped. What's more, since the Coast Guard did not know the exact position of the craft, patrollers were forced to conduct a nighttime search over an enormous area. In short, there is no reason to believe that the *Witchcraft* fell under the deadly spell of the Devil's Triangle.

Martians,

Zombies, and

Fabricated

Feathers

"THE WAR OF THE WORLDS" BROADCAST

- - - -

October, 1938, panic rips through the United States. Dramatizing H. G. Wells's novel, the Mercury Players create a national frenzy with what would become the infamous "War of the Worlds" broadcast. Feeding on the public's credulity, the broadcast—which started out as an innocent performance with a svelte citizen named Welles behind the microphone—quickly became one of the most famous ruses in the history of hoaxes.

Orson Welles Traumatizes a Nation!

The Mercury Players never intended to deceive anyone. They announced from the start that the realistic-sounding newscast of the Martian invasion was strictly fictive, repeating the warning three times *during* the broadcast. Yet scores of people panicked: They packed their bags, ran into the streets in their nightclothes, piled furniture on top of their cars, and held wet handkerchiefs over their faces to ward against extraterrestrial gas attacks. Switchboards were swamped, police stations were crammed with crowds, and traffic ground to a halt.

Radio Liars. What made them swallow the story hook, line, and sinker? In those halcyon days—before truth in advertising was considered an oxymoron and quiz shows disenchanted a nation—people *believed* what they heard on the radio. Late in 1938, radio was just beginning to come into its own as a source for "on the spot" news. H. V. Kaltenborn and Edward R. Murrow had recently begun broadcasts from Vienna and London about Hitler's warlike intentions. In short, the public trusted radio; in fact, the most quoted response from people who were later asked *why* they panicked was "I knew it was true because I heard it on the radio newscast."

Orson Welles never intended to deceive anyone.

Duped and Delighted!

Newspaper articles about the incident—numbering more than 12,500—continued for three weeks. The public spoke out, writing letters to the Federal Communications Commission (FCC) and to the radio station WABC. And they weren't all miffed about the hoax that wasn't a hoax: 40 percent of the letters to

the FCC spoke out in favor of the broadcast, while letters to WABC—which had a tie-in to all the CBS network stations across the country—ran 1,086 in favor, and 684 against the show. Meanwhile, back at the Mercury Theater, 1,450 letters flooded in, with a whopping 91 percent in favor of the program. What's more, the "War of the Worlds" debacle actually had a positive outcome: Taking a lesson from the public's panic, authorities learned how better to prepare for emergencies—perhaps even Martian invasions—in the future.

Panic in South America!

Most writings about "The War of the Worlds" broadcast have overlooked two later incidents that took place in Santiago, Chile, when the play was broadcast there in November 1944, and in Quito, Ecuador, where the show aired on the radio in February 1949. Santiago was in a panic—with terrified victims suffering injuries and heart seizures—and the situation in Quito was even worse. The public panicked, and then learned that they'd been duped. Angry rock-throwing crowds surrounded the building that housed the radio station and newspaper; soon, the building was in flames, and it was nearly destroyed. At least twenty people died in the fire, many of whom jumped from upper story windows where the radio station was located. The Ecuadorian government responded by arresting some of the rioters as well as the director of the newspaper and the two writers of the modified radio script. The charges: Inciting a riot. The South American "newscasts," it seems, did little to caution listeners that the broadcast was bogus.

ZOMBIES
- - - -

Carnival of Souls, Night of the Living Dead, I Walked with a Zombie, Chopper Chicks of Zombietown: We're all familiar with celluloid zombies who, cursed by some crazy voodoo magic, return to plague the world they left behind. Quaint folklore, but hardly fact. But when Wade Davis, an ethnobotanist at Harvard, announced the results of his field work in Haiti, many nonbelievers sat up straight. A bestseller that was later made into an unfaithful movie, *The Serpent and the Rainbow* lent credibility to the myth of the undead.

The Walking Dead Watch Their Salt!

Trouble was, the zombies that Davis and others discovered weren't really dead; they just *seemed* dead, thanks to a drug-induced cataleptic state. Buried and dug up again, they miraculously "returned to life." According to author Bernard Diederich, whose article "On the Nature of Zombie Existence"

appeared in a 1983 issue of *Caribbean Review,* the Haitian psychiatrist Lamarque Douyon reported on at least three cases of what seem to be genuine zombies—hapless Haitians who were poisoned by bocors (witch doctors) at the request of a family member. A round-trip ticket to the world of the undead, it seems, is issued as punishment for something that the zombie-recruit did or didn't do. The poison—absorbed through the skin or through a cut in the skin—produces a slow paralysis that lowers the body's metabolic rate. Trapped within an immobile body, staring through eyes whose pupils are fixed and dilated, the victim—whose heartbeat becomes virtually indiscernible—remains *conscious.* Only an electroencephalogram belies the victim's beating heart.

Burial is short and sweet. After more than eight hours underground, the undead may become real dead. As the potential zombie is dug up, onlookers join in a ceremony, beating the earth above the casket with sticks in order to prevent the victim's spirit from returning to his or her body. Back in the world of the living, the zombie must adhere to a strictly salt-free diet in order to maintain that certain living-dead countenance. It seems that salt (and possibly other drugs) can bring the victim—whose mind functions at a very low level—back to some semblance of normalcy. Eventually, victims may recover most of their mental functions. So next time someone tells you he walked with a zombie, don't assume he's crazy; he just might be telling the truth.

Toad's Skin, Puffer Fish, and Creeping Paralysis:

Wade Davis tried for quite some time to get a sample of the powder that produces a zombie's paralysis. Defrauded by some bocurs, he eventually obtained what was *probably* authentic powder. Analysis showed that it contained hallucinogenic extract of a toad's skin, hallucinogenic extract of the plant Datura stromonium, and tetrodotoxin, an extract of puffer fish (also known as fugu fish). Tetrodotoxin is a powerful nerve toxin that produces a creeping paralysis, and is usually fatal by itself; the other ingredients in the powder apparently moderate its effects. Sounds like voodoo magic, but it's possible that the ingredients in zombie powder might have uses in modern medicine, especially surgery; with this in mind, scientists have been studying the compounds.

ARCHEOPTERYX
- - - -

In a Bavarian quarry in 1861, the first fossil of what would later be called Archeopteryx—"the ancient wing"—was discovered. The piece of slate, when split, appeared to have the imprint of a pigeon-sized dinosaur on both sides. The dinosaur—then called Compsognathus—showed clear marks of a long feather tail, wings, and other feather imprints.

Winged Creature
Flies in the Face of Fossil Frame-up!

In 1862, Karl Haeberlein, a German physician, sold the fossil to the Natural History section of the British Museum. An expensive investment, the purchase was largely supported by anatomist Richard Owen, the director of the museum, who also happened to be bitterly opposed to Charles Darwin—the man who ruffled many a feather with his ideas about evolution. Clearly a transitional form between reptiles and birds, the pint-sized dinosaur strongly supported the theory of evolution. It did not, however, especially support *Darwin's* two-year-old version of the origin of things.

For more than a century, experts accepted Archeopteryx as a bona fide fossil—feathers and all. But in 1985, astronomer Fred Hoyle and his coauthor, Chandra Wickramasinghe, scandalized the scientific community: The original archeopteryx fossil and another fossil found a year later in the same quarry, the authors announced in the *British Journal of Photography,* were *forgeries.* Actually, according to Hoyle, it wasn't the fossils that were forgeries—it was the *feathers.* They were added, he claimed, by grinding up the same rock, making it into a paste, then applying it to one side of the fossil imprint, and pressing feather impressions into it.

Feathers and Facts: Three more recently discovered fossils of Archeopteryx (found in the 1950s) also showed feather impressions, although not as distinctly. The fossils also showed other distinctly bird-like features, such as a "wishbone," a perching foot, and a retro-verted pubis (a tilted-back pelvic bone). In short, the British Museum's findings established that the Archeopteryx fossil was not simply a dinosaur that had been decked out in faux feathers.

Birds of a Feather?

Hoyle—who did not have access to the original fossil—claimed that the hoax was designed to discredit Darwin and Thomas Henry Huxley, another adamant supporter of the theory of evolution. Hoyle's theory assumed that the instigator—whom the astronomer identified as Richard Owen—was motivated by his opposing ideology: Owen, Hoyle argued, was a card-carrying creationist. If Huxley enthusiastically supported the far-flung fossil, then Owen could step in to expose the ruse, thus discrediting Huxley, and by implication, the theory of evolution.

But Hoyle's claim had a few flaws. Owen, it seems, was *not* a creationist. Rather, as Stephen Jay Gould convincingly demonstrated in his article "The

Archeopteryx Flap," which appeared in a 1986 issue of *Natural History,* the museum director was an evolutionist—although not the same sort of evolutionist as Darwin and Huxley. What's more, the British Museum conducted extensive tests of the original Archeopteryx fossil. Using a scanning electron microscope, they found that the fossil was not a forgery: Exactly matched hairline cracks on the surfaces of both halves of the fossil block of stone showed that the two surfaces had not been tampered with; there were no traces of any "cement" (the alleged paste made from ground rock) on either half of the stone slab; and the two halves of the slab fit together perfectly, showing that no material had been added to either half. The Archeopteryx fossil was indeed a genuine transitional form that showed the characteristics of both reptiles and birds.

Index